TURKEY AFTER THE JULY COUP ATTEMPT

HEARING

BEFORE THE

SUBCOMMITTEE ON EUROPE, EURASIA, AND EMERGING THREATS

OF THE

COMMITTEE ON FOREIGN AFFAIRS
HOUSE OF REPRESENTATIVES

ONE HUNDRED FOURTEENTH CONGRESS

SECOND SESSION

SEPTEMBER 14, 2016

Serial No. 114–222

Printed for the use of the Committee on Foreign Affairs

Available via the World Wide Web: http://www.foreignaffairs.house.gov/ or
http://www.gpo.gov/fdsys/

U.S. GOVERNMENT PUBLISHING OFFICE

21–542PDF   WASHINGTON : 2016

For sale by the Superintendent of Documents, U.S. Government Publishing Office
Internet: bookstore.gpo.gov   Phone: toll free (866) 512–1800; DC area (202) 512–1800
Fax: (202) 512–2104   Mail: Stop IDCC, Washington, DC 20402–0001

COMMITTEE ON FOREIGN AFFAIRS

EDWARD R. ROYCE, California, *Chairman*

CHRISTOPHER H. SMITH, New Jersey
ILEANA ROS-LEHTINEN, Florida
DANA ROHRABACHER, California
STEVE CHABOT, Ohio
JOE WILSON, South Carolina
MICHAEL T. McCAUL, Texas
TED POE, Texas
MATT SALMON, Arizona
DARRELL E. ISSA, California
TOM MARINO, Pennsylvania
JEFF DUNCAN, South Carolina
MO BROOKS, Alabama
PAUL COOK, California
RANDY K. WEBER SR., Texas
SCOTT PERRY, Pennsylvania
RON DeSANTIS, Florida
MARK MEADOWS, North Carolina
TED S. YOHO, Florida
CURT CLAWSON, Florida
SCOTT DesJARLAIS, Tennessee
REID J. RIBBLE, Wisconsin
DAVID A. TROTT, Michigan
LEE M. ZELDIN, New York
DANIEL DONOVAN, New York

ELIOT L. ENGEL, New York
BRAD SHERMAN, California
GREGORY W. MEEKS, New York
ALBIO SIRES, New Jersey
GERALD E. CONNOLLY, Virginia
THEODORE E. DEUTCH, Florida
BRIAN HIGGINS, New York
KAREN BASS, California
WILLIAM KEATING, Massachusetts
DAVID CICILLINE, Rhode Island
ALAN GRAYSON, Florida
AMI BERA, California
ALAN S. LOWENTHAL, California
GRACE MENG, New York
LOIS FRANKEL, Florida
TULSI GABBARD, Hawaii
JOAQUIN CASTRO, Texas
ROBIN L. KELLY, Illinois
BRENDAN F. BOYLE, Pennsylvania

AMY PORTER, *Chief of Staff*   THOMAS SHEEHY, *Staff Director*
JASON STEINBAUM, *Democratic Staff Director*

———

SUBCOMMITTEE ON EUROPE, EURASIA, AND EMERGING THREATS

DANA ROHRABACHER, California, *Chairman*

TED POE, Texas
TOM MARINO, Pennsylvania
MO BROOKS, Alabama
PAUL COOK, California
RANDY K. WEBER SR., Texas
REID J. RIBBLE, Wisconsin
DAVID A. TROTT, Michigan

GREGORY W. MEEKS, New York
ALBIO SIRES, New Jersey
THEODORE E. DEUTCH, Florida
WILLIAM KEATING, Massachusetts
LOIS FRANKEL, Florida
TULSI GABBARD, Hawaii

CONTENTS

Page

WITNESSES

LETTERS, STATEMENTS, ETC., SUBMITTED FOR THE HEARING

APPENDIX

TURKEY AFTER THE JULY COUP ATTEMPT

WEDNESDAY, SEPTEMBER 14, 2016

HOUSE OF REPRESENTATIVES,
SUBCOMMITTEE ON EUROPE, EURASIA, AND EMERGING THREATS,
COMMITTEE ON FOREIGN AFFAIRS,
Washington, DC.

The subcommittee met, pursuant to notice, at 2:25 p.m., in room 2200, Rayburn House Office Building, Hon. Dana Rohrabacher (chairman of the subcommittee) presiding.

Mr. ROHRABACHER. Let me go on record right off the bat by saying how happy I am that Congressman Meeks and I decided to have haircuts on the same day. All right. Okay.

I call this hearing to order. Just over 2 months ago, this subcommittee met for a hearing focused on Turkey's democratic decline, the second such hearing that has been held by this committee. Eight days later, an attempt was made to overthrow the AKP government, and during the chaos and conflict on the night of July 15, over 240 Turkish civilians were killed, and the Turkish Parliament bombed from the air.

As one might expect, this and the following upheaval that followed it has been a traumatic experience for the people of Turkey. Let them have no doubts, however, that the United States stands by them in our support for democracy and the rule of law. President Obama has made that clear on July 15, and that remains the case.

Unfortunately, great damage has been done, and great damage has been done as part of the coup attempt, but, at the same time, President Erdogan has been making a bad situation worse by using the failed coup as an opportunity to expand his own political power. In short, after the coup collapsed, a state of emergency was declared, and the government began arresting a wide range of opponents that had nothing to do with the coup. Journalists, secularists, military officers, government officials who did not agree with President Erdogan's vision for Turkey, they were arrested, 10,000 of them, and they have been arrested, and a number of them have been tortured.

The Turkish Government is blaming its travail on—and I can't pronounce his first name—Fethullah Gulen. Okay.

Mr. WEBER. Fethullah Gulen.

Mr. ROHRABACHER. There it is.

A Turkish religious philosopher living in exile on a Pennsylvania farm. The claim that he personally planned and ordered the coup has been accepted by many Turkish citizens despite the lack of substantial evidence to indicate that. To this effect, I don't find such charges to be credible, and I believe that the Turkish Government has erred by proclaiming anyone and everyone involved in the Gulenist religious movement to be part of a conspiracy that put on the coup.

Again, over perhaps 100,000 civil servants, military officer, teachers, policemen, prosecutors, even judges have been removed from their jobs and many of them have been arrested. They have been replaced by Erdogan's cronies, by political opportunists, and, yes, by even Muslim Brotherhood radicals and other Islamic fascists. As one example of how far these ridiculous purges have gone, the Turkish soccer authorities announced they have fired 94 officials, including a number of soccer referees, for their ties to the coup. Over 20,000 people—whatever that exact number, it is in the tens of thousands—have been arrested, and the Government of Turkey has used this coup to settle old scores and to clean out the house of those it does not seem—or deem sufficiently loyal to Erdogan's vision for Turkey.

Incredibly, it was reported last month that Turkey would release 38,000 criminals from prison to make room for those taken into custody in these purges, letting murderers, rapists, thieves go in order to make room for political opponents. It doesn't get much worse than that.

As we have in our conversations about recent events in Turkey, I want to underline my desire to see Turkey become an economically strong partner of the United States that is at peace both at home and with its neighbors. The Turks have been wonderful allies of the American people. And as we are going through this testimony today and we are seeing what the current regime in Turkey is doing, which is heavy handed and wrong—let's not forget that the Turkish people themselves have been so loyal to us. We must wish them well and do what we can to try to help them through this confusing time period. I mean, Turkey, as I say, needs, in order to do that and to—and for us to succeed and for them to succeed, Turkey needs to have strong democratic institutions, a free press, and a country in which people abide by the rule of law.

The government's current witch hunt that sees disloyal Gulenists behind every door is bound to backfire, even in the short run, but be disastrous in the long run. The fear and tension created by a thuggish coup and by a heavy-handed response does not and is not serving the Turkish people well.

I want to thank our witnesses for appearing here today. And, without objection, their written statements will be made part of the record, and all members will have at least 5 legislative days to submit additional written questions or extraneous materials for the record.

I now turn to our ranking member, Mr. Meeks, for his opening statement.

Mr. MEEKS. Thank you, Chairman Rohrabacher, for calling today's hearing on Turkey and giving us an opportunity to discuss the attempted coup and its consequences for Turkey and the United States and Turkey's relationship.

Clearly, the coup was a traumatic shock to the system. I can recall when it was taking place looking at my television screen in disbelief. So it is clear, and I agree with Mr. Rohrabacher in this aspect, I stand in solidarity with the democratically elected Turkish Government and against any violent attempts to overthrow it or any other democratically elected government. Democracy is important. We can't have coups d'etat. We have got to speak out against coups d'etat in order to have democratic order.

When I think about over 270 people were killed as the Parliament and ministries were attacked with helicopters and F-16s joining the fight, I can't even imagine such a scene here in Washington, DC, soldiers firing into civilian crowds. We cannot, and I can't believe as Members of Congress that that is something that we want to see or can condone in any way. It is our job to respect and defend the democratic process, and a democratic Turkey is in everyone's best interests.

Following the failed coup, there has been a big issue of Mr. Gulen, his residency in Pennsylvania, and his movement's involvement in the coup. And it has taken on an increasingly charged role in Turkish-U.S. relations. The United States has taken the accusations and requests for Mr. Gulen's extradition and detention very seriously, but as I say, in democracies, there are processes. There are institutions, and there is a judicial process that is in place now and a related treaty that will determine this outcome. So it is not something that could be done arbitrarily or capriciously or anything of that nature. There is a process that has to be had and should be. That is the reason why we have these institutions, and that is the reason why we have these treaties.

So I say just linking the U.S. Government to the coup, apart from being false, damages our important relationship, and it is something that I deeply care about because the relationship between the United States and Turkey is very important. I understand that members of the Turkish Government are understandably angry, but emotional statements and accusations will not expedite the judicial process. It has to run its course, as our judicial system demands.

And perhaps, as a result of the failed coup and subsequent purges, Turkey has markedly stepped up its fight against Daesh in Syria. Turkey is a NATO ally and plays an essential role in the region, and has sought to mend relations with Russia and Israel. And while cooperation with those countries is welcome, Turkey's role in NATO and as host to over 1,500 U.S. troops remains especially important to the United States Congress.

In our previous hearing on this topic we discussed Turkey's democratic development, the Kurdish question, and the role of a civil society in Turkey. During the failed coup and afterwards, in an impressive show of unity, all Turkish political parties came to the defense of the elected government and even supported a search for those allegedly responsible for the coup, including Gulenists and members of Hizmet movement. Indeed, those found guilty should be rooted out of the government's organs and brought to justice.

The state of emergency, however, must not be used to cover, to detain, arrest, and fire those with no responsibility for the coup. How many judges, teachers, and businessmen have been found innocent and allowed to return to their posts? We must look at and analyze because if you had nothing to do with this and you are found innocent, as I am sure there are many individuals, they should be returned to their posts. Furthermore, are members of the legal pro-Kurdish movement, the HDP, being unjustly ensnared in a political war? As previously mentioned, we must protect the United States-Turkey relationship and simultaneously encourage strong democratic institutions and respect for the law.

So, for me, this is an important hearing to listen to these witnesses, to get your expert viewpoints on what is or is not taking place in Turkey, because it is important for us to decide as Members of the United States Congress what we should or should not do, what we should or should not say.

Just as I say that, the Turkish Parliament should not do things based upon emotion, I also believe that we in the United States Congress should not do something just based upon emotion. We need to try to figure out what the issues are and what the facts are, and move accordingly because it is important for our relationship, and I think all over the world that the U.S. and Turkey have a strong relationship.

So I want to thank the witnesses in advance for their testimony, and I look forward to asking questions as we move forward. And I yield back.

Mr. ROHRABACHER. I thank you, Mr. Meeks.

One of our members also has a 1-minute opening statement, Colonel Cook from California.

Mr. COOK. Thank you very much, Mr. Chair.

I think a number of us are worried about Turkey. Obviously, this is a Foreign Affairs Committee hearing. I am also on the House Armed Services Committee. I am also on the NATO Parliament. As already discussed, everybody knows that Turkey has been a key ally. It is a member of NATO. The Turkish Americans in my district throughout California, very, very close to the business climate, all those pluses. I think right now everybody is very, very nervous about the Erdogan government, some of the things that are happening as we speak, obviously, the relationship with the Kurds, the relationship with some of the Christians. And I am not sure—right now, I don't have that optimism about Mr. Erdogan. And this was well before the coup. And this is going to determine whether our military relations continue. We have a key base at Incirlik. We had problems before. We are going to see what happens after the coup. And we also have an impending sale of F-35s, the most advanced aircraft. And whether that will still be approved by the administration and Congress, that is something that is coming up.

So this coup and everything that has happened there, I am not as optimistic as my colleagues because of some of the mixed signals, but then you look at Israel, that a year or 2 years ago, they had severed diplomatic relations, and surprisingly enough, recently they have kind of normalized relations with Turkey.

So, hopefully, we can get passed this, hopefully we can establish a dialogue with Mr. Erdogan, and hopefully, we can have a democracy in a country right now where, in my opinion, it does not exist.

Thank you very much, Mr. Chairman.

Mr. ROHRABACHER. Today, we have four excellent witnesses. And my direction would be, as usual, if you could get to the heart of the matter and give us 5 minutes of the basic information you think we need to know. The rest of your statement will be made part of the record. And we will proceed with that in mind.

And our first witness—and I will introduce all witnesses, and then you will testify—Nina, and, again, I am going to pronounce this, Ognianova? That is good enough? All right. And she is the coordinator for Europe and Central Asia programs for the Committee to Protect Journalists, where she has tracked developments in Turkey for the past several years. Previously, she worked as a writer for the International Journalists Network and earned a master's degree from Missouri School of Journalism.

And next is Alan Makovsky, who is a senior fellow at the Center for American Progress. He has been with us several times, and I am finally learning how to pronounce his name. It is a private think tank, of course, the Center for American Progress, and it is here in Washington, DC. And for more than a decade, he served as a senior professional staff member right here, so we give him a little leeway that way, on the Foreign Affairs Committee of the House Foreign Affairs Committee, covering the Middle East, Turkey, and the other problems that we tackled in this committee. Before that, he directed the Washington Institute's Turkey Research Program and was an employee of the State Department.

We have next Ahmet Yayla. Good. Got it. And he is an adjunct professor at the Department of Criminology, Law, and Society at George Mason University, and the deputy director of the International Center for the Study of Violent Extremism. He has a long career as a Turkish law enforcement officer and served as chief of the antiterrorism division of the Turkish National Police. And he has earned his master's degree and Ph.D. Degrees from the University of North Texas. And he is the author of a recent book, and I would ask you to give us the title of your book during your testimony. See? There you go. Okay.

And then there is Aaron Stein, a senior fellow at the Atlantic Council's Rafik Hariri Center for the Middle East—Hariri, okay—where this institute follows and comments on developments in Turkey and in the region. Dr. Stein received his Ph.D. In Middle East and Mediterranean studies at King's College in London.

Does that mean you are English?

Mr. STEIN. No. American.

Mr. ROHRABACHER. Oh, there. All right.

So we will start on this end, and we will then, after 5-minute presentations, open it up for questions from the panel. Okay. Thank you.

STATEMENT OF MS. NINA OGNIANOVA, COORDINATOR, EUROPE AND CENTRAL ASIA PROGRAM, COMMITTEE TO PROTECT JOURNALISTS

Ms. OGNIANOVA. Mr. Chairman and members of the subcommittee, thank you for the opportunity to testify on press freedom in Turkey after the July 15 coup attempt. My name is Nina Ognianova, and I am the Eurasia program coordinator at the Committee to Protect Journalists. We are a press freedom organization dedicated to defending the rights of journalists worldwide, and it is an honor to speak with you today.

My oral statement will be a summary of my written statement, which contains extended analysis and specific examples of press freedom violations in Turkey.

On July 15, military officers attempted to overthrow Turkey's elected government. Thousands of Turks took to the streets to defend it, and more than 200 were killed. In this crucial moment, Turkey's usually polarized society was united. The AKP received overwhelming support from across the political spectrum, but instead of channeling that support to bridge differences, authorities have been using the failed putsch to purge their opponents: Mounting a sweeping crackdown on the critical media when Turkey most needs a plurality of voices. The government immediately blamed the coup on the Hizmet movement, followers of preacher Fethullah Gulen, whom the Turkish Government accuses of leading a terrorist organization. Gulen has denied all accusations.

Within days after the putsch, the AKP announced the state of emergency that allowed it to govern by decree. Within a few weeks, the government had closed down more than 100 media, including broadcasters, newspapers, magazines, publishers, and distribution companies, and it had detained over 100 journalists. At least 30 news Web sites were censored by state regulators. Some journalists have managed to escape into exile. Others' passports were canceled to prevent their departure. Judges suspected of having ties to Hizmet were purged and replaced with AKP loyalists.

The Prime Minister's office has revoked the press credentials of over 600 journalists. In mid-August, CPJ's 2016 International Press Freedom Award recipient, Can Dundar, resigned his editorship of the daily Cumhuriyet and said he would not return to Turkey while the state of emergency was in effect. Trusting the judiciary, Dundar said, would be like laying one's head on the guillotine.

The scope of the purge has spread far beyond the requirements of the safety and security of the Turkish state. With all the media outlets perceived as tied to Gulen already shuttered and with the list of journalists arrested for once having worked at this media growing by the day, the purge has now moved on to individual critics of both the government and the Hizmet movement, and the longstanding judicial and police harassment of the Kurdish media has intensified.

The state of emergency has given security agencies the right to detain individuals for up to 30 days without access to a judge, which has created conditions in which detainees are at risk of abuse. In my written testimony, I have described several cases of reported police abuse of journalists in custody, and all of these abuses have been carried out with impunity.

CPJ is dismayed at the cancellation of a growing number of journalists' passports. This punitive measure has been extended to the family members of the accused. In one disturbing recent case, on September 3, Can Dundar's wife, Dilek, here in the picture, was prevented from traveling to Europe to visit her husband in exile. Security officers confiscated her passport without giving any reason. She has not been charged with a crime, so the only explanation for this official action is that she is being punished for her husband's journalism.

There is much that remains unclear about the July 15 coup attempt, but instead of allowing Turkish journalists to do their job and to investigate the truth about this conspiracy, the government is making the press pay the price for the illegal actions of rogue military officers.

Turkey's domestic purge of its media has international repercussions. Credible independent media reports are vital for the world's understanding of Turkey's handling of the Syrian refugee crisis or the battle against Islamic State.

While it is important to condemn the coup attempt, we strongly urge U.S. leaders to condemn the continuing purge of opposition and independent media. The U.S. should allow Turkish journalists caught in the post-coup purge to travel to the United States. CPJ awardee Can Dundar hopes to travel to New York in November to receive his award. The U.S. should not honor Turkish arrest warrants for journalists and should encourage other countries not to honor those warrants as well and should treat journalist's travel documents as valid even if Turkey has already canceled them. We urge Congress to consider imprisoned Turkish journalists as prisoners of conscience, including the more than 100 journalists detained in the aftermath of the failed coup.

Plunging to a naked authoritarianism risks destabilizing Turkey, which is a vital U.S. ally. Putting an end to the ever broadening crackdown on independent media is a vital step toward stopping and reversing that plunge before it becomes too late.

Thank you for providing CPJ with the opportunity to address you today.

[The prepared statement of Ms. Ognianova follows:]

Testimony before the House Foreign Affairs Committee's Europe, Eurasia, and Emerging Threats Subcommittee

Submitted by Nina Ognianova
Europe and Central Asia Program Coordinator
Committee to Protect Journalists

to the

United States House of Representatives Committee on Foreign Affairs
"Turkey after the July Coup Attempt"
Wednesday, September 14, 2016

Chairman Rohrabacker, Ranking Member Meeks, and members of the subcommittee:

Thank you for the opportunity to testify on press freedom in Turkey in the aftermath of the failed coup attempt on the night of July 15. My name is Nina Ognianova, and I am the Europe and Central Asia Program coordinator of the Committee to Protect Journalists (CPJ), an independent, nonprofit organization dedicated to defending press freedom and the rights of journalists worldwide. It is an honor to speak with you today, and I appreciate the opportunity to address this committee on behalf of CPJ.

In my written testimony before this subcommittee, submitted on July 13, two days before the attempted coup in Turkey, I said that the Turkish government's crackdown on the media had reached an unprecedented intensity. But in the two months that have elapsed since then, Turkey's offensive against independent or critical media has gone into overdrive, with more than 100 journalists detained, more than 100 media outlets shuttered, hundreds of press workers stripped of their credentials, and many others forced into exile—all to the detriment of a public in need of independent news at a critical time.

In this testimony, I will highlight some of the most urgent press freedom issues in Turkey. I would like to caution the subcommittee that the numbers cited here are a snapshot only, taken at the time of writing. With conditions on the ground constantly evolving, I urge the subcommittee to regularly reference CPJ's "Turkey Crackdown Chronicle" for brief daily updates on the latest attacks on press freedom in the country.

In this testimony, I will also provide recommendations to the U.S. government on how to assist Turkey's beleaguered journalists and to help improve conditions for media in Turkey. Unless otherwise specified, all data cited in this testimony is based on CPJ research.

INTRODUCTION

On July 15, rogue military officers attempted to overthrow Turkey's elected government. Thousands of Turkish citizens took to the streets to defend the government; more than 200 people lost their lives. In this crucial moment, Turkey's usually fragmented, polarized society was united. The government of the ruling Justice and Development Party, or AKP, received overwhelming support from across the political spectrum. But instead of channeling that support to bridge differences, the government has been using the failed putsch to purge its opponents, mounting a sweeping onslaught against the critical media when Turkey most needs a plurality of voices.

The government immediately blamed the attempted coup on the Hizmet movement—followers of preacher Fethullah Gülen, whom the Turkish government accuses of leading a terrorist organization and "parallel state structure" in Turkey from his self-imposed exile in the United States. Gülen denied these accusations.

The crackdown on Gülenists—including on media perceived to have ties to the Hizmet movement—had been ongoing for months, but the coup attempt created a pretext for its acceleration. Within days after the attempted coup, the AKP announced a state of emergency that allowed it to govern by decree, overstepping judiciary and parliamentary scrutiny. Within a few weeks, the government had closed down more than 100 broadcasters, newspapers, magazines, publishers, and distribution companies; and it had detained more than 100 journalists. At least 30 news websites were censored by state regulators. Some journalists managed to escape to exile. Others' passports were cancelled to prevent their departure. Judges suspected of having ties to the Hizmet movement were purged and replaced with AKP loyalists. The prime minister's office revoked the press credentials of more than 600 journalists.

In mid-August, CPJ 2016 International Press Freedom Award recipient Can Dündar publicly resigned his editorship of the daily *Cumhuriyet* newspaper and said he would not return to Turkey while the state of emergency was in effect. Dündar, who has criticized both the AKP and its former ally, the Hizmet movement, in the past, argued that the government is exploiting the failed coup to eliminate all its opponents and to redesign the judiciary for its own purposes. Trusting such a judiciary, Dündar said, would be like "laying one's head on the guillotine."

KEY PRESS FREEDOM ISSUES

MASS DETENTION OF JOURNALISTS, REPORTS OF ABUSE IN CUSTODY

The scope of the purge has spread far beyond the requirements of the safety and security of the Turkish state. With all media outlets perceived to have ties to the movement already shuttered, and the list of journalists arrested for once having worked there growing by the day, the purge has moved on to individual journalists who have criticized the government and the Hizmet movement. The longstanding judicial and police harassment of Kurdish media has sharply intensified.

Within a week of the announcement of the state of emergency, Turkish police detained at least 48 journalists and shuttered three news agencies, 16 television stations, 23 radio stations, 45 newspapers, 15 magazines, and 29 publishing houses and distribution companies by decree. The decree stipulated that, going forward, any cabinet member could order the closure of any media organization if he or she deemed it "a threat to national security."

The state of emergency gives security agencies broad rights to detain individuals for up to 30 days without access to a judge and with restricted access to a lawyer. These measures, along with Turkey's temporary suspension of its obligations under the European Convention on Human Rights, according to the Council of

Europe Commissioner for Human Rights Nils Muižnieks, have created conditions in which detainees are especially at risk of abuse.

Indeed, allegations of police abuse of journalists in custody surfaced almost immediately. On August 10, police beat four journalists detained near the scene of a bomb attack that day in the southeastern city of Diyarbakir: Hasan Akbaş, Fırat Topal, and Serpil Berk of the daily *Evrensel*, and freelance photographer Sertaç Kayar. Their lawyer said the journalists told him they were at a nearby café when the bomb went off, so they rushed to the scene, took photographs and video, and left. Police stopped them at a checkpoint, forced them out of their vehicle, made them kneel, and handcuffed them. The journalists said they waited for roughly an hour and a half in this position while the police hit them, swore at them, and threatened them, saying, "If anyone lifts his head, shoot him in the head," and "Is this the press? You should shoot them." The four journalists were later released. The officers who beat them remain unpunished.

Similarly, several journalists detained by police on August 16 described after their release having been beaten and verbally abused in custody. Reporters with the pro-Kurdish daily newspaper *Özgür Gündem*, DIHA news agency, and broadcaster IMC TV said officers "beat all of us while our hands were bound behind our backs," according to *Özgür Gündem*'s Sinan Balık. Other journalists from the group described being "hit with the butt of a gun," and "subjected to beatings and insults for 36 hours," being kneed in the face, and being "pushed down the stairs from the second floor." At least one of the journalists—all of whose extended personal accounts are available online as part of CPJ's "Turkey Crackdown Chronicle"—said she lost consciousness due to the blows. Another journalist, IMC TV reporter Gülfem Karataş recounted being threatened with rape, subjected to racist slurs, and being whipped with a chain. No police officer has faced criminal or disciplinary action.

CANCELLATION OF PASSPORTS, RETALIATION AGAINST FAMILY MEMBERS

CPJ is dismayed at the cancellation of a growing number of journalists' passports, in some instances without any prior notification to the holders. We are appalled that this punitive measure has been extended to family members of the accused.

On August 9, Istanbul's 14th Court of Serious Crimes ordered authorities to cancel the passports of six staff members of the embattled pro-Kurdish daily newspaper *Özgür Gündem*. Former editors-in-chief Eren Keskin and Hüseyin Aykol, former responsible news editor Reyhan Çapan, writers Ayşe Berktay and Reyhan Hacıoğlu, and lawyer Nuray Özdoğan, who has also written for the newspaper, face terrorism charges because of the newspaper's coverage. They are now trapped in Turkey.

The incident took place three days after passport control officers at Istanbul's Atatürk airport briefly detained broadcast journalist Hayko Bağdat as he re-entered Turkey, and confiscated his passport without an explanation.

While the exact number of invalidated passports remains undetermined, dozens of journalists who have been put under investigation on unsubstantiated accusations of ties with coup plotters have been banned from travel. Others, who happened to be traveling when their passports were invalidated, have been unable to move freely.

On July 27, for instance, Sevgi Akarçeşme, former editor-in-chief of the shuttered English-language daily *Today's Zaman*, was taken off a plane traveling from Brussels to New York, where she was to begin a journalism fellowship at the City University of New York. Shortly after boarding, she said, airline personnel escorted her off the plane and explained to her that her Turkish passport had been cancelled. She was unable to make her planned U.S. trip.

Perhaps even more disturbing is a September 3 incident involving Dilek Dündar, the wife of prominent Turkish journalist and CPJ International Press Freedom Award recipient Can Dündar, who was prevented from traveling from Istanbul to Europe to visit her husband in exile. Security officers at Istanbul's Ataturk airport confiscated Dilek Dündar's passport without giving a reason. She has not been charged with any crime and, to her knowledge, she is not under investigation. "The government has taken my wife hostage," Can Dündar told CPJ after the incident. "This is an example of Turkey's authoritarian rule—in our new 'judicial' order, if one is put on trial, the whole family is on trial."

JOURNALISTS AND 'STATE SECRETS'

A number of recent prosecutions of high-profile investigative journalists illustrate the failure of Turkish authorities to respect the role media play in a democracy. Instead of accepting, even reluctantly, that the press will cover stories of national and international interest and importance, Turkish prosecutors have relied on overbroad laws to treat such coverage as treason.

Most recently, on September 2, Istanbul's 13th Court for Serious Crimes began hearing the case of four prominent journalists from the defunct daily *Taraf* on charges relating to an elaborate alleged conspiracy, codenamed "Balyoz (Sledgehammer)."

Ahmet Altan, Yasemin Çongar, Yıldıray Oğur, and Mehmet Baransu are charged in connection with the case. Baransu was a columnist at *Taraf* in 2010, when the daily published a series of articles alleging that Turkish military officers were planning to bomb mosques in the country and to shoot down a Turkish warplane in order to spark conflict with Greece and destabilize the then newly elected Justice and Development Party (AKP) government. Baransu also co-authored a book with Tuncay Opçin, who is also on trial in the case, which was published in 2012 and outlined several alleged military conspiracies.

In 2010, when the AKP and the Hizmet movement were in a tacit alliance against the military and security service's role in politics, *Taraf* was lauded as the publication that broke the Sledgehammer story. But in today's environment, the journalists are being sued for divulging state secrets because of that same story. The independence and professionalism of the proceedings against the journalists has been marred by an indictment that contains portions obviously copied and pasted from another case, that of former *Cumhuriyet* editor Can Dündar. So sloppy have prosecutors been in preparing the *Taraf* indictment that they failed to remove Dündar's name from the pasted text: The indictment refers to him as the defendant though he is not a defendant in this case, according to multiple reports. The *Taraf* trial is scheduled to resume in late November.

In perhaps the most well-known case of recent months, Dündar and Erdem Gül, *Cumhuriyet*'s Ankara bureau chief, were tried and convicted of revealing state secrets that could harm the security of the state, and sentenced to seven years in prison (reduced to five years and 10 months), and six years in prison (reduced to five years), respectively. The charges stem from a May 2015 *Cumhuriyet* report that alleged Turkey's intelligence service sought to send weapons to rebel groups in Syria under the guise of humanitarian aid. The report was embarrassing to the government, and President Recep Tayyip Erdoğan publically pledged that he would punish Dündar for what he considered an act of treason. On May 29, 2015, the same day *Cumhuriyet* published the story, Erdoğan said he had filed a criminal complaint against the daily. "The only thing that matters to them is casting a shadow on Turkey's image," Erdoğan said in a June 1, 2015, broadcast on the state broadcaster. "I suppose the person who wrote this as an exclusive report will pay a heavy price for this... I will not let him go." By November that year, Dündar and Gül were imprisoned. They spent 92 days in jail before the Turkey's highest court ordered them released pending trial. Prosecutors initially lodged treason charges against them, but abruptly dropped those charges days before the trial began. They are currently free, pending appeal, though Dündar has gone into exile.

Erdoğan's high-pitched rhetoric against Dündar may have put the journalist in physical danger. On May 6, a man shot at the editor twice as he spoke with reporters during a break in his trial. "Traitor!" the assailant shouted, before pulling the trigger. Dündar was not hurt, but a television journalist at the scene was injured by a stray bullet.

"We do not know who the attacker is, but we know who made us into a target," Dündar said afterwards.

PRO-KURDISH MEDIA PERSECUTED, SHUT DOWN

If there is one specific journalistic community in Turkey that has for years been targeted with punitive actions by the government, both before and after the coup attempt, it is the pro-Kurdish press. Reporters with such pro-Kurdish media outlets as the Dicle News Agency (DİHA), the all-female Jin News Agency (JİNHA), the daily *Özgür Gündem*, the Kurdish-language daily *Azadiya Welat*, or the television station IMC TV have consistently been detained, imprisoned, and hit with multiple trumped-up criminal charges. Their employers' websites have been blocked, their licenses revoked, and their print runs have been confiscated. One editor died of injuries sustained while covering a military incursion into a predominantly ethnic-Kurdish town.

Before the purge of pro-Hizmet movement media began, it was the Kurdish outlets that had been the most frequently prosecuted under Turkey's overly broad laws anti-terrorism legislation, which has been interpreted to criminalize a wide range of news coverage as aiding and abetting groups Turkey has classed as terrorists.

With the cleansing of Turkey's media landscape of outlets perceived as sympathetic to Gülen almost complete, the anti-press campaign is moving to eradicating pro-Kurdish publications.

One recent example stands out: On August 16, Istanbul's Eighth Court of Penal Peace ordered the country's oldest pro-Kurdish newspaper, *Özgür Gündem*, to temporarily stop publishing. The court did not say for how long. According to an ostensible copy of the court order published on Twitter by the volunteer journalist collective 140journos, prosecutors accused the daily of producing propaganda for the Kurdistan Workers' Party (PKK), which the Turkish government classes as a terrorist organization. The court order also accused the paper of incitement to insurrection and publishing articles that threaten the security and territorial integrity of the state. Police raided the newspaper's offices and detained at least 17 of the daily's journalists. Four other journalists with the news outlets DİHA and IMC TV were also detained for covering the raid on *Özgür Gündem's* newsroom. All but two of the detained journalists were released without charge, but they reported being beaten, threatened, and verbally assaulted in custody. A third *Özgür Gündem* journalist—a columnist and a member of the publishing board, was additionally arrested. She, too, complained of mistreatment in prison.

When the socialist weekly *Atılım* subsequently ran special daily editions produced by *Özgür Gündem* journalists under the shuttered daily's logo, an Istanbul court immediately ordered all future such special editions confiscated from newsstands.

As with pro-Hizmet movement media, which the government accuses of aiding a terrorist organization, pro-Kurdish media are also labeled as supporting terrorist groups --- in this case, the PKK. In both cases, the Turkish government fails to make the distinction between criminal activity and covering a banned group or criticizing government policies. Journalism that the government does not welcome is prosecuted as terrorism.

CONCLUSION AND RECOMMENDATIONS

There is much that remains unclear about the July 15 coup attempt in Turkey. It is unknown who the masterminds were, how the operation was organized, how deep and wide the conspiracy ran, and how the plotters managed to keep it a secret. Instead of embracing press freedom and allowing Turkish journalists to do what they do best – investigating and uncovering the truth about this conspiracy – the government is making journalists pay the price for mutinous military officers' unlawful actions. Turkey is burying the truth deeper by eradicating the country's independent and opposition media, imprisoning or forcing the journalists who ask tough questions out of the country, often discarding even the pretense of due process, rule of law, or transparency.

Turkey's domestic purge of its media has international repercussions. Credible, independent media reports are vital to the world's understanding of Turkey's handling of the Syrian refugee crisis, or the battle against the Islamic State group.

While it is important to condemn the coup attempt of July 15, we strongly urge Turkey's international partners, specifically the United States, to condemn the continuing purge of opposition and independent media that has followed the attempted coup.

Public, unequivocal statements condemning the crackdown on the press and calling for its immediate reversal are especially important now as fear and self-censorship take hold in the face of a staggering arrest campaign. We urge congressional leaders to stress the crucial role that pluralistic media play in times of crises in their meetings with Turkish officials, and to urge other U.S. officials to stand up for Turkey's beleaguered journalists both publicly and privately as well.

The United States should allow Turkish journalists caught in the post-coup purge to travel to the United States. CPJ International Press Freedom Awardee Can Dündar hopes to travel to New York to receive his award on November 22. The United States should not honor Turkish arrest warrants for journalists, should encourage other countries not to honor those warrants, and should treat journalists' travel documents as valid, even if Turkey has cancelled them.

We urge Congress to consider imprisoned Turkish journalists as prisoners of conscience, including the more than 100 journalists detained in the aftermath of the failed putsch.

We urge Congress to advise Turkish lawmakers and officials on reforming counterterrorism legislation to protect the press and to scrap Article 299 of the Penal Code, which criminalizes insulting the president. Congress should further call on Turkey to allow the press to cover fighting between the military and ethnic-Kurdish youth in the country's southeast, and to cease prosecuting journalists on anti-state charges.

In Turkey on August 24, U.S. Vice President Joe Biden said that Turkey has no greater friend than the United States of America. Good friends can still offer plainspoken advice and frank criticism. A Turkish plunge into naked authoritarianism risks destabilizing Turkey, a vital U.S. ally. Putting an end to the ever-broadening crackdown on independent news media is a vital step toward stopping and reversing that plunge before it is too late.

Thank you for providing CPJ with the opportunity to address this important matter.

Mr. ROHRABACHER. Thank you very much.

Mr. Makovsky.

STATEMENT OF MR. ALAN MAKOVSKY, SENIOR FELLOW, CENTER FOR AMERICAN PROGRESS

Mr. MAKOVKSY. Thank you. Thank you, Mr. Chairman. Chairman Rohrabacher, Ranking Member Meeks, esteemed members of the subcommittee——

Mr. ROHRABACHER. Put the mike a little closer to you. There you go.

Mr. MAKOVKSY. Yeah. I forgot to turn it on. Second time in a row I have done that.

Mr. ROHRABACHER. How much you forget.

Mr. MAKOVKSY. Yeah. I told you I wasn't on this side of the table before. Anyway, I will start again.

Chairman Rohrabacher, Ranking Member Meeks, esteemed members of the subcommittee, it is an honor to have been invited back to testify here today on this important topic. Maybe I will get it right this time.

Mr. Chairman, any discussion of the post-coup environment in Turkey must begin with an acknowledgement that Turkish society endured an enormous trauma on July 15, as you and the ranking member and Mr. Cook all said in your opening remarks. As well, I think we should acknowledge that the U.S. and, for that matter, European Union's response to the coup was less than optimal, inadvertently feeding conspiracy mindedness in Turkey.

That said, it is now 2 full months since the coup, and it is more than fair to take stock of the Turkish Government's reaction. Their reaction has been found wanting in three major ways. First of all, the vastness and persistence of the purge of the civil service, which you have detailed in your opening remarks, the arrest of journalists, the closure of media outlets, the arrests for spurious reasons, many of these arrests having nothing whatsoever—of people having nothing whatsoever to do with Gulen or Gulenists, has turned a somewhat understandable initial desire to err on the side of caution into an unbridled witch hunt. Even President Erdogan recently expressed some concern about how vast this is, and he said to governors: You should not vie with one another to see who can arrest more people.

And this is happening against a background of growing authoritarianism in Turkey that predates the coup attempt, as we discussed at our previous hearing.

Second, even in ostensibly pursuing post-coup unity, President Erdogan's approach has been divisive. Revulsion of the coup attempt and justifiable pride in thwarting it through popular action united many Turks in the coup's immediate aftermath. However, government-led post-coup efforts at healing were, in fact, themselves divisive, excluding the party that most Kurds in Turkey's southeast support, the People's Democracy Party, or HDP, which is in fact, the third largest party in Parliament. For example, HDP has been excluded from talks on a new Turkish constitution, and it was excluded from the emotional August 7 Istanbul rally that attracted millions of Turks supporting democracy and condemning the coup.

Third, the Turkish Government has engaged in anti-U.S. scapegoating following the coup attempt, primarily through means of the heavily pro-government media, which has repeatedly blamed the coup attempt on the U.S. Government and various U.S. citizens, both public and private. The government has reinforced this scapegoating by raising suspicions regarding Fethullah Gulen's long-time residence in the United States and by leading the Turkish public to expect the United States to deliver Mr. Gulen to Turkey quickly, with little acknowledgement that extradition is a lengthy process that can only be successfully achieved with hard evidence.

According to a generally reliable Turkish poll taken during the third week of August, one-quarter of Turks believe that the United States was behind the coup whereas 55 percent believe Gulen was the mastermind. That means one-quarter believe we were much more behind it than even Gulen. Anecdotal evidence, I would say, however, suggests that far more than one-quarter believe the U.S. had at least indirect involvement in or prior knowledge of the coup attempt. According to the same poll, 90 percent of Turks now have an unfavorable view of the U.S., with only 9 percent favorable.

Looking ahead, it is clear that President Erdogan is now a far more dominant ruler than he was even before the coup attempt. He is also likely to remain a difficult partner for the United States. I don't believe Turkey wants to leave NATO, nor should we want it to do so, but President Erdogan's Turkey is likely to push the boundaries of partnership at times and use its reborn relationship with Russia as well as manipulate anti-Americanism at home as leverage with us on bilateral issues.

Two final points quickly, Mr. Chairman, if I may. A good relationship with Turkey remains a highest priority U.S. national interest, but we should not turn a blind eye to Turkey's deteriorating human rights situation nor conveniently forget that this deterioration began well before the July 15 coup attempt.

Second, and finally, more broadly, we must remain alert to the possibility that Turkey could indeed drift from the Western alliance. I do not believe that will happen, but given the many strains on U.S.-Turkish bilateral relations, the possibility of Turkey turning away from the West is now sufficiently plausible that it would be wrong not to plan for that contingency.

Thank you, Mr. Chairman.

[The prepared statement of Mr. Makovsky follows:]

TESTIMONY OF ALAN O. MAKOVSKY
SENIOR FELLOW, CENTER FOR AMERICAN PROGRESS
HOUSE COMMITTEE ON FOREIGN AFFAIRS,
SUBCOMMITTEE ON EUROPE, EURASIA, AND EMERGING
THREATS
HEARING: "TURKEY AFTER THE JULY COUP ATTEMPT"
SEPTEMBER 14, 2016

Chairman Rohrabacher, Ranking Member Meeks, Esteemed Members of the Subcommittee:

It is an honor to have been invited to testify today on this important topic. With your permission, I would like briefly to discuss six basic issues related to "Post-Coup-Attempt Turkey":

THE COUP

The July 15 coup attempt in Turkey was a nationwide trauma for Turkey. The details are well-known by now. More than 270 people killed and more than 2,000 wounded; aerial bombings of the nation's capital Ankara, including the Parliament building; soldiers fighting police and soldiers fighting soldiers in Istanbul and elsewhere throughout the nation; and the revelation of the deepest sort of factionalism in the military that historically was the nation's most trusted institution. And, in the early days after the coupists seemingly had been vanquished, it wasn't completely clear that the coup was truly over. The coup also assaulted the national pride of the many Turks who were convinced that the era of coups – the feature of Turkish political history that most distinguished Turkey, unhappily, from its NATO allies -- had ended for good.

Any discussion of the coup and its aftermath must start with basic understanding of that near-nationwide trauma. In response to a coup attempt, any government would tend to err on the side of over-reaction in pursuit of plotters and putschists. After all, a coup is not simply a protest demonstration; it is an assault on a regime.

U.S. RESPONSE

As the U.S. and EU responded to the military and civil service purge that followed the coup, our shock at the breadth of the purge seemed to many Turks to overwhelm our condemnation of the coup itself, our sympathy for Turkish society for having endured it, and our relief that the duly elected government had prevailed. I think we could have done a better job of balancing our reaction. The fact that we did not do so fed conspiracy-mindedness in Turkish society and made even our strongest friends and supporters in Turkey uneasy.

TURKISH RESPONSE

It is now almost two full months since the coup, and it is more than fair to take stock of the Turkish government's reaction. That reaction has been found wanting in three major ways: 1) **Over-zealous purge.** The vastness and persistence of the purge has turned what may initially have been a somewhat understandable initial reaction into an unbridled witch-hunt. Almost immediately after the coup was quashed, the Turkish government determined, or decided, that the blame for the coup lay with military followers of Fethullah Gulen, a Muslim preacher who has been living in self-imposed exile in the United States since 1999 and whose organization, known as Hizmet, includes a vast international array of schools, hospitals, and other institutions.

Rather than focusing its wrath strictly on the military coupists, however, the Turkish government chose to expunge Gulenist influence from the entire civil service and, to the extent possible, all Turkish society. As a result, more than 100,000 civil servants have been fired or suspended and more than 40,000 arrests have occurred since the coup attempt. People are being arrested for owning books by Gulen or for having made deposits in a bank owned by Gulenists. Adherence to Gulen's stated philosophy, which has nothing to do with coups or violence, is sufficient cause for job dismissal or worse.

Turkey has set out fifteen very broad criteria for these arrests when there should be only one: involvement in the coup attempt.

In addition to the purge of civil servants – including tens of thousands of teachers – more than a hundred journalists have been arrested and more than 2,000 fired. Many of the journalists being hounded merely wrote for Gulenist-owned newspapers and, as the net widens, many have no Gulenist association whatsoever. In addition, the government has shut down three news agencies, sixteen television stations, twenty-three radio stations, forty-five newspapers, fifteen magazines, and twenty-nine publishing houses – most, but not all, Gulenist-associated.

Gulenist institutions and private businesses owned by Gulenists also have been dissolved or taken over by the state. A Turkish official recently claimed that some $4 billion in Gulenist-associated property has been seized.

And, of course, all this is happening against a background of growing authoritarianism in Turkey that pre-dates the coup attempt, as we discussed at our previous hearing.

2) Divisiveness. Government-led post-coup efforts at healing were, in fact, divisive, excluding Kurds – or, at least, excluding the party that most of the Kurds in Turkey's southeast support, the Peoples' Democracy Party (HDP, in Turkish). For example, Turkish President Recep Tayyip Erdogan instructed that court cases against parliamentarians be dropped, except those directed at HDP members. This is the case, even though HDP – like the other opposition parties – condemned the coup immediately, and its parliamentary caucus huddled with other parliamentarians inside the parliament building as the coupists' bombs rained down on that building and elsewhere in the parliament compound. More recently, the leader of Turkey's largest opposition party, the secularist, center-left Republican People's Party (CHP), called the purge a "witch-hunt" that has gone way beyond capturing Gulenists to engulf a variety of Erdogan critics, including social democrats, leftists, and Ataturkists.

3) Anti-U.S. scapegoating. The pro-government media has repeatedly blamed the coup attempt on the U.S. government and various U.S. citizens, public and private. One Turkish cabinet minister, now holding the all-important interior portfolio, blamed the U.S. government directly, and another said the U.S. had prior knowledge of the coup attempt and didn't warn the Turkish government. More recently, at the G20, President Erdogan thanked President Obama for opposing the coup, but the damage done to popular attitudes toward the U.S. is likely to be immense. The government has re-inforced these attitudes by raising suspicions about Gulen's long-time residence here and leading the public to expect the U.S. to deliver Gulen to Turkey quickly, with little acknowledgement that extradition is a lengthy process that can only be successfully achieved with hard evidence.

According to a generally reliable Turkish poll taken during the third week of August, one-quarter of Turks believe the United States was behind the coup, whereas 55% believe Gulen was the mastermind. Anecdotal evidence, however, suggests that far more than one-quarter believe the U.S. had at least indirect involvement in the coup through its hosting of Gulen.

GULEN AND GULENISTS

It is impossible now to separate a discussion of Turkey's post-coup response from consideration of the nature of the Gulen movement itself and its alleged role in the coup. As we discussed at the last hearing, there are two hallmarks of the Gulenist movement that have significantly and positively distinguished it from many Islamic movements, particularly the radical movements with which we've become all-too-familiar in this century and, for that matter, in decades previous: The Gulenist movement establishes schools that emphasize science and math rather than religion, and it preaches a message of peace and inter-faith comity.

However, there is now a considerable body of circumstantial evidence suggesting that there is another side to this movement, a secret side that has exploited the institutions of the Turkish state in order to pursue its enemies. That side apparently showed itself in the Ergenekon and Balyoz trials, which led to the destruction of hundreds of military and other careers – careers that couldn't be revived in most cases even after evidence was proved fraudulent and convictions were overturned. It also robbed many of these same innocent people of years of their lives, as they endured prison and, reportedly

in some cases, torture. There is also circumstantial evidence –
strong circumstantial evidence -- to suggest that those trials
opened pathways for promotion for other followers of the
movement.

Yet, widespread skepticism outside Turkey about the
government's coup accusation against Gulenists is
understandable. The Turkish government's all-too-quick
determination that Gulenists were culpable seemed a bit too
convenient. Erdogan had been attacking Gulen and Gulenists
since his government was made the target of a corruption
probe in December 2013, which Erdogan believes was an effort
by Gulenist prosecutors to drive him from office. The fact that
Erdogan's first step the day after the coup was to fire 2,745
judges only re-inforced the impression that he was using the
coup to go after his enemies – an impression further re-
inforced by the ongoing purge of civil servants.

Furthermore, some 40% of Turkey's generals and admirals
were arrested or simply relieved of their duties as a result of
the coup. Thousands of other military officers have been
arrested as well. The Turkish government doesn't say that all
of them are Gulenists but the implication is that most are. To

believe Gulenists had penetrated the leadership ranks of the military so thoroughly is to believe that hundreds if not thousands of religious Gulenists held to a conspiracy for more than two decades, moving up the ranks of an institution devoted to secularism and committed to opposing Gulenism. If it's true – and perhaps it is – it's certainly the conspiracy to end all conspiracies.

Even were the conspiracy indeed proven true regarding some of Gulen's followers, that would not prove that Gulen himself gave the order for the coup attempt. That issue will be considered in the extradition case Turkey is preparing against Gulen.

ERDOGAN UNASSAILABLE

It is clear that Erdogan is now a far more dominant ruler even than he was before the coup attempt. He rules by emergency law. He enjoys considerably bolstered popular backing born of his leadership against the coup. For the first time, according to a respected poll, a plurality of Turks favor Erdogan's idea of a "strong Presidency." His assault on the Gulenists is widely supported not only by his own traditional base but by secularists as well. And he has taken advantage of popular revulsion at the coup attempt finally to bring the military to heel, putting its military school system under the ministry of education, its university-equivalent War Academy under the state's Higher Education Council, and its hospitals under the ministry of health and generally ending the military's status as a closed-caste system that runs its own schools and makes its own rules. That will allow the government to influence admissions to cadet schools and the academy to an unprecedented degree and lay the groundwork for a very different, presumably more socially conservative officer corps -- and one fully responsive to civilian leadership.

Erdogan seems also to have won the chastened and presumably weakened military leadership over regarding Syria policy. Long reported as resistant to intervening directly in Syria, the military complied with Erdogan's orders and moved tanks and special forces into Syria on August 24; they are still there and are likely to be so for some time. Of course, in this case, the military leadership may have shared with Erdogan a desire to demonstrate to the region as well to fellow Turks that the military remains a force to be reckoned with in the post-coup-attempt era.

TURKEY: EAST, WEST, OR IN-BETWEEN?

And where is Turkey headed for the near and medium term? Despite the revival of the Erdogan-Putin flirtation – and despite ongoing disputes with the U.S. over extradition of Gulen and over U.S. cooperation with the Syrian-Kurdish, PKK-associated militia YPG -- I believe Turkey's preference will be to remain within the Western community of nations. Turkey's military, whatever its composition, is likely to continue to appreciate the benefits, strategically and educationally, of NATO membership. Economically, Turkey is structurally linked to the West. Nearly half its trade is with the EU (45% of its exports and 38% of its imports in 2015), which is also the source annually of roughly two-thirds its foreign direct investment.

Turkey's remaining in NATO and fundamentally tied to the West is the good news here – or, at least, the optimistic projection. The less optimistic one is that Turkey will remain an often independent player within NATO – an ally but an ally that pushes the boundaries of partnership. In a recent speech in the U.S., Turkish Deputy Prime Minister Numan Kurtulmus rhetorically asked whether Turkey is "changing its axis," meaning from alignment with NATO to alignment with Russia.

"Turkey never changes its axis," he said. "Turkey has only one axis, and it is its own." That statement captures much of the spirit of Turkish foreign policy under Erdogan, sovereigntist but within NATO.

It should also be the U.S. preference that Turkey remain within NATO and within the Western community. Turkey is geostrategically important to the United States, and that importance is naturally heightened when we are fighting a war, as we are now, against ISIS. Turkey's status as a prominent Muslim-majority nation in NATO also serves our interests in many ways, as well as Turkey's.

We will face challenges, however. For one, using Turkish military facilities and convincing Turkey's leaders and the Turkish public of our commitment to their security, while calling Turkish leaders out on mounting human rights violations at the same time, is a tricky business. It is a balance we must find, however. We cannot turn a blind eye to Turkey's deteriorating human-rights situation nor conveniently forget that this deterioration began well before the July 15 coup attempt.

Second, and more broadly, we must remain alert to the possibility that Turkey could indeed drift from the Western alliance. As I've indicated, I do not believe that will happen, but the possibility is now sufficiently plausible that it would be wrong not to plan for that contingency.

Thank you, Mr. Chairman.

Mr. ROHRABACHER. Thank you for that important warning.
Next, we have Mr. Yayla.

STATEMENT OF AHMET S. YAYLA, PH.D., DEPUTY DIRECTOR, INTERNATIONAL CENTER FOR THE STUDY OF VIOLENT EXTREMISM

Mr. YAYLA. Thank you very much, Chairman Rohrabacher, Ranking Member Meeks.

Mr. ROHRABACHER. And we would like you to speak right into that microphone.

Mr. YAYLA. Okay. Dear Chairman Rohrabacher, Ranking Member Meeks, members of subcommittee, and ladies and gentlemen, it is an honor to testify before you today. Since we have 5 minutes, I have detailed in my written statement, but I would like to go over a few quick points very fast.

I think it is critical to understand the pre-coup conditions in Turkey, especially in regards to President Erdogan. The economy before the coup was suffering very deeply. The tourism industry was almost dead after the several terrorist attacks. After the shootdown of Russian airplane, the sanctions put on Turkey by Putin were deteriorating. The economy was very bad, especially tourism suffered a lot. And after 2013 December criminal charges against the government, the rule of law had started to mean nothing, and several international businessmen, businesses and investors left Turkey, like Tesco, PayPal, also. And freedom of speech, free media, and the rule of law started to mean nothing in Turkey, basically eroding the foundations of democracy in Turkey.

Turkey was going through tough times, and the relationship with the West, with the EU, and NATO was deteriorating. Erdogan, as the gatekeeper of ISIS, kept tricking the EU with the sending of several thousand refugees to the European countries. The U.S. was upset with Turkey's failed commitment to fight with ISIS and Erdogan's, or Turkey's, illicit support to ISIS. For example, the leader of Turkish ISIS, Halis Bayancuk, was released from prison almost a year ago, and right now, he freely operates inside Turkey without any problems.

Just a week ago, suspects of Sultanahmet's Blue Mosque ISIS suicide attack were released from prison. If you look at the arrests of those ISIS people, ISIS suspects, when they got arrested somehow they were not handcuffed, but if you look at the journalists, when they got arrested, they were handcuffed from the back. So that is the approach of the government, unfortunately. If you compared the ISIS members and the journalists or other people getting arrested.

Another problem was the Zarrab case. Right now, Zarrab, an Iranian Turkish businessman, in New York Federal—being tried in New York Federal court, and he was the key person to Turkey's oil-to-gold scheme, which was managed by the government and Zarrab was managing that, and right now is being tried for money laundering, bank fraud, and evading sanctions against Iran. And that person was arrested during 2013, corruption charges raised by Istanbul police, who Erdogan backed up very furiously and who pledged to Erdogan's wife's foundation millions of dollars.

Close associates of Erdogan and his sons were being named with dealing with ISIS oil on the media, and Erdogan could not produce a diploma, university diploma, which was being circulated on social media against him. It was very obvious that Erdogan was not able to reach his goal through democratic means with all those troubles, as the polls showed that his support was diminishing.

When we look at the aftermath of the coup, I have spent almost 20 years as a chief of counterterrorism operations in Turkey, and I know the capacity of government officials and counterterrorism of the police. As the police was dealing with the coup attempters, the security services and intelligence, all of a sudden, after 3 hours, Erdogan left Ataturk Airport. We had a list of 1,653 military officers who were deemed as the perpetrators of the coup, and of whom almost 90 percent were not on the field. And all of a sudden, the security services in 3 hours found ways to investigate the coup attempt. They analyzed the evidence they had. They made a list of 1,653 military officers all over Turkey. They got warrants for those officers and distributed those warrants to 81 provinces all over Turkey in 3, 4 hours. And then the police somehow started to arrest those people in their homes or at their vacation places. And from a technical perspective, it should take months, not weeks. So it is very clear that that list was prearranged. And also we can see that from a list of prosecutors and judges who were fired. They fired immediately 2,000 something prosecutors. One the prosecutors was deceased 57 days at the time of his firing. So they fired someone who died 2 months ago.

And we can see a lot of examples of that. For example, Saygi Ozturk, a prominent journalist. We listed a few of them. The list the government had when they were firing the judges and prosecutors was prepared almost 2 years ago because the cities where they were working were the cities where they were working 2 years ago.

Another important aspect involves the purge, firing, and arrests. Over 100,000 people were fired, and almost 60,000 people were arrested and detained. And nobody knows how those lists were arranged and how those people were involved in the coup.

Another important factor is the questions and inconsistencies of the statements of important people after the coup. For example, the chief of staff, Akar, the Turkish national intelligence director came out and said that he informed Akar at 4 p.m. About the coup. However, Akar himself, he was sitting in his office up until 9 p.m. When he was—until he was arrested. He did not inform Erdogan. He did not inform the Prime Minister nor did he inform his commanders of the air force, army. The air force commanders learned about the coup at a wedding in Istanbul. The commander of Gendarmerie learned about the coup in Ankara at a wedding. So this is a very questionable act on not letting know his superiors, President Erdogan and the Prime Minister and others.

I would like to finish, as I am out of time. My book's name is ''ISIS Defectors: Inside Stories of the Terrorist Caliphate.''

And I would like to finish with one note. My son was arrested after I wrote an article on this issue in Turkey because my passport was canceled, and the charges against my son is—the reason that he was arrested was because my passport was canceled.

And I would like to give a story from the prophet Muhammad. One companion of the prophet Muhammad asked the prophet Muhammad, ''What is the biggest jihad?'' Because nowadays, with ISIS, we hear a lot of stories about jihad. The prophet Muhammad said, ''A word of truth in front of a tyrant's ears.''

Thank you.

[The prepared statement of Mr. Yayla follows:]

House Foreign Affairs Subcommittee on Europe, Eurasia, and Emerging Threats

TURKEY AFTER THE JULY COUP ATTEMPT

September 14, 2016

Ahmet S Yayla, Ph.D.

Deputy Director

International Center for the Study of Violent Extremism (ICSVE)

Turkey's July Coup Attempt: "A Gift from God" to a new Authoritarianism

The July 15, 2016 unsuccessful "coup" attempt in Turkey happened in the midst of exceptionally stressful times when Turkish President Recep Tayyip Erdogan was going through both domestic and international crises which are essential to understand and better analyze how the so-called coup came about. In fact, as Erdogan himself addressed his supporters at the Ataturk airport just a few hours after the coup attempt, he called the coup *"a gift from God"* and later it became clear—that it provided the rationale for solving his many troubles and most importantly, the perfect opportunity to completely wipe out his growing opposition as he quickly grabbed authoritarian rule at a level he would never be able to attain through democratic means.

Pre-Coup Conditions

The political and economic atmosphere in Turkey before the coup was extremely difficult for President Erdogan. Turkey was going through turmoil for a variety of reasons. The economy was struggling, with the tourism industry almost collapsing in response to losing millions of tourists due to worsening security concerns following several terrorist attacks around the country. In addition, Russian President Vladimir Putin introduced economic sanctions on November 2015[1] for Turkey after the shoot down of the Russian warplane causing Turkey to lose one of its primary trade partners and source of tourism. Furthermore, several international investors (i.e. PayPal and Tesco) have left Turkey seeing what happened after the December 2013 corruption operations which reached up to the highest echelon's of Erdogan's government and which he promptly crushed by arresting the police involved. The rule of law in Turkey had started to mean nothing causing international investors to quaver. Several large media outlets (i.e. Koza Ipek Media) were also shut down or confiscated by Erdogan, key journalists were arrested, this beginning even years before the coup attempt, and the freedom of speech and free media were being attacked on a daily basis, eroding the foundations of democracy in the country.

One of the most important factors of course was Turkey's distancing itself from the West as a NATO member. Relationships between the EU and Turkey have been suffering due to the fact that Erdogan as the gatekeeper of ISIS kept threatening the EU with the release of hundreds of thousands of refugees and then demanding money and visa-free travel for the Turks. This had followed years of unsuccessful

---

[1] *"Vladimir Putin announces Russian sanctions against Turkey"*
https://www.theguardian.com/world/2015/nov/28/vladimir-putin-calls-for-greater-sanctions-against-turkey

attempts of Turkey to accede to the EU. Ties with the U.S. were also weakened due to Turkey's failure of real support to the Coalition forces against ISIS and other terrorist organizations and the illicit support given to the regional terrorist organizations in Syria including ISIS and al-Nusra. Turkey has unfortunately become the main hub and logistical support base for ISIS, allowing members to operate freely in its borders to provide all the logistical and military needs from Turkey without any interruptions and let its fighters pass back and forth through Turkish borders[2]—including allowing 38,000 foreign fighters from over one hundred nations stream into ISIS via Turkey.

In fact, the Turkish government consistently releases the suspects of ISIS cases around the country with surprisingly little investigation or judicial review while it was at the same time cracking down hard on journalists and political activists. Turkey is the leader in the world for jailed journalists. In 2016 alone number of the arrested journalists reached to 117[3] apart from the journalists who were detained and released. Before the coup Turkey was already one of the lead nations for the number of jailed journalists, yet ISIS members and supporters in Turkey consistently evade prison. For example, on January 12, 2016, ISIS carried out a suicide attack near the Blue Mosque in Istanbul killing twelve German tourists. This attack's case was tried in Istanbul court and recently during the latest trial, half of the arrested suspects were unexpectedly released[4]. Similarly, Turkish ISIS leader Halis Bayancuk was released from prison in Manisa along with ninety-four other ISIS suspects[5]. Bayancuk openly supports ISIS on his social media accounts and operates freely in Turkey. The support Turkey has extended to ISIS and other terrorist organizations has distanced itself from the West and isolated itself not only in the region but almost in the entire world having only few friendly countries left.

Another troubling headache of Erdogan was the Zarrab *"oil for gold"* money laundering case that resurrects the December 2013 internal Turkish corruption case that Erdogan crushed. Iranian Turk, Reza Zarrab, who was arrested upon his entry into the U.S. on March 19, 2016 is currently held behind bars in New York and facing federal charges for his role in Turkey's Iranian *"oil to gold"* scheme. Zarrab is accused of evading sanctions against Iran, conspiracies to commit money laundering and bank fraud of millions of dollars through the Turkish banking system[6]. His U.S. federal court trial is set to start soon and Erdogan must be paralyzed with fright that Zarrab is going to testify about his and his family's as well as high government officials' roles in the over 100 billion dollars of *"oil to gold"* money scheme Zarrab is accused of arranging[7]. It is expected that Zarrab is going to reveal how this system worked and how the highest levels in the Turkish state along with some Turkish banks were behind his crimes.

In fact, Zarrab was arrested in December 2013 in Istanbul, along with several key people very close to Erdogan for similar charges as a result of Turkish Police corruption operations. Erdogan managed to

---

[2] *"Deadly Interactions"* by Ahmet S Yayla. http://www.worldpolicy.org/deadly-interactions

[3] *"Turkey's Press Crackdown Unparalleled in Recent History"* http://www.turkeytms.com/2016/09/08/turkeys-press-crackdown-unparalleled-in-recent-history/

[4] *"Marshall Law is not Applied to ISIS"* http://www.shaber3.com/iside%ADohal%ADislemiyor%ADhaberi/1271107/

[5] *"All Suspects Released at ISIS Trial"*
http://www.cumhuriyet.com.tr/haber/turkiye/503898/ISiD_Davasi_nda_tum_saniklar_tahliye_edildi.html

[6] *"Turkish National Arrested for Conspiring to Evade U.S. Sanctions Against Iran, Money Laundering and Bank Fraud"* https://www.justice.gov/opa/pr/turkish-national-arrested-conspiring-evade-us-sanctions-against-iran-money-laundering-and

[7] *"U.S. Wants to Keep Charged Turkish-Iranian Businessman Reza Zarrab in Custody"*
http://www.wsj.com/articles/u-s-wants-to-keep-charged-turkish-iranian-businessman-reza-zarrab-in-custody-1464208901

crush and hide these operations from sight at the time by arresting the police officers and prosecutors involved. In 2013, the arrests were made on similar charges of money laundering and bribery but Erdogan managed to turn the case around and deemed it as a coup plot against himself by the police officers involved, which also provided him rational for the complete overhaul and purging at that time of the Turkish (National) Police and Judiciary system. Inside Turkey in 2013, Zarrab was very quickly released after receiving open support by Erdogan claiming that he was an honorable businessman and charitable source—as Zarrab had donated millions of dollars to *Erdogan's wife's* charity organization![8] Furthermore, Erdogan was never able to explain why and how he had at that time over one billion dollars of cash at his home in Istanbul. It was clear that he, with his son and daughter, were trying to hide that money as the police operations were carried out. His son in fact, clumsily handled affairs and ending up with bungled money transfers showing up in the press—press that Erdogan attacked and shut down soon after. As the Zarrab Federal case in New York starts to further towards a full-scale trial, we will hear more details on the involvement of Erdogan and the Turkish banking system some of which were made public during the corruption charges carried out by the Istanbul Police—unless the U.S. government allows some plea bargain to occur which prevents Zarrab from testifying against the Turkish President, a player who the West so desperately needs at this time as an ally in the fight against ISIS. This would indeed be a troubling development and allow Erdogan once again to evade paying the price of serious corruption.

Additional troubles for Erdogan were the ISIS oil deals in which it was revealed after the Russian plane was shot down that ISIS was selling oil directly to Turkey and profiting Erdogan's son[9]. Turkey and Erdogan's close circles have repeatedly been openly criticized on facilitating the sale and transportation of ISIS oil[10]. Upon the attack on the Russian plane, several reports and satellite images were released on how this scheme worked. Moreover, in a recent letter[11] written to the UN Security Council, it was detailed how ISIS oil was being transported by BMZ Group Sea Transportation and Construction Company, owned by Erdogan's son Bilal Erdogan, against whom there is also a pending money laundering trial in Italy[12].

Furthermore, domestically Erdogan was having hard times and struggling with the issue of not being able to produce his college diploma. Erdogan to this day could not produce a four-year university diploma to the public which is a constitutional requirement for serving as President of Turkey. Just before the coup attempt, several different copies of clearly fake diplomas were being circulated in the social media by his supporters as a proof of his graduation. However, it was clear that the diplomas were

---

[8] *"Turkish First Lady's Charity Got Millions from Accused Fraudster"*
http://www.bloomberg.com/news/articles/2016-05-26/turkish-first-lady-s-charity-got-millions-from-accused-fraudster
[9] *"Russia, Turkey trade accusations over who bought oil from ISIS"* http://www.cnn.com/2015/12/02/europe/syria-turkey-russia-warplane-tensions/
[10] *"Russian Letter to UNSC Claims Erdogan's Family are Directing the Smuggling of ISIS Oil!"*
http://www.huffingtonpost.com/aydoaean-vatanda/russian-letter-to-unsc-cl_b_9502784.html
[11] *"Russia unveils 'proof' Turkey's Erdogan is smuggling Isis oil across border from Syria"*
http://www.independent.co.uk/news/world/europe/russia-releases-proof-turkey-is-smuggling-isis-oil-over-its-border-a6757651.html
[12] *"Bilal Erdogan: Italy names Turkish president's son in money laundering investigation allegedly connected to political corruption"* http://www.independent.co.uk/news/world/europe/bilal-erdogan-italy-investigates-turkish-presidents-son-over-money-laundering-allegedly-connected-to-a6879871.html

fabricated as the numbers did not match or the signatures of the professors were wrongly recorded (i.e. their academic titles were not correct for the time the academician signed the diploma).

Erdogan, while struggling with all of the aforementioned issues, was pushing hard for constitutional changes that would consolidate his authority as a President and would provide him continued immunity from prosecution as long as he held office. However, he had been losing ground in Turkey as polls prior to the coup showed weakening support towards the idea of a constitutional change. *It was obvious that he would not be able to reach to his goal through democratic means.*

The coup attempt took place in the midst of these political and economic instabilities at a time when Erdogan needed immediate solutions. Consequently, the coup which was most certainly staged came as a savior for Erdogan as he himself openly stated it was *"a gift given by God to him"*. In fact, he was very upfront about this from the beginning of the coup attempt and immediately started to consolidate all the powers he needed, he could not access in the past, because they were not in the constitution. With the coup attempt, Erdogan was able to appeal powerfully to national sentiment and unity while no one could raise any voice against him or would dare to question any of his policies—particularly so after the purges and widespread arrests began.

Uncertainties and Reservations about the Coup Attempt

From the start of the coup attempt until today, there are many crucial unanswered questions and occurrences which cannot be explained logically. To begin with, the coup attempt started at 10 p.m. in the evening. Turkey has experienced several coups in its past and the military is knowledgeable of when and how to carry them out. Indeed, the Turkish military historically has been regarded as the guardian of democracy. Under normal circumstances, people usually do not go to bed before midnight in Turkey and especially in the major cities the streets are alive till midnight. All the past coups happened around 3 to 4 a.m., early in the morning while people were asleep. The beginning of the coup from this perspective was very questionable for having any hope of succeeding. It would be very hard to keep coup actions a secret when television, radio and people themselves were all active observers. Some pro-AKP media argued that the coup was set into motion early in the evening because it had been uncovered and the coup attempters had to rush into carrying out their plans. However, the facts defy this, since the coup attempt was reported by the Turkish National Intelligence to the Military Chief of Staff around 4 p. m., yet there were not any counter measures taken to prevent them from carrying out the coup attempt[13].

Furthermore, the coup attempters failed to restrict communications. The Internet was not restricted and people kept communicating through social media, and cell phone networks worked without any problems or interruptions. Normally in a coup, the Internet and the mainstream media would be shut down. On the contrary, from the beginning of the coup until the end, almost all media were broadcasting live—leading one to conclude that the plotters wanted the coup actions to appear in media rather than be hidden from it until they had successfully secured power. The only media initially restricted was Turkish State Radio and Television which were not the only major media outlets at the time and later on CNN-Turk was raided by a number of soldiers and the broadcasting was interrupted

---

[13] *"Why didn't the Turkish National Intelligence Inform the Chief of Staff on Time"*
http://www.cumhuriyet.com.tr/haber/turkiye/571482/MiT__darbe_girisimini_neden_haber_vermedi__Hakan_Fid an_MGK_de_cevap_verdi.html

around one hour[14]. It is clear that the coup attempters did not want to totally silence the media simply because if they really wanted to shut down broadcasting, they would deploy serious forces to do so.

The coup plotters also failed to arrest almost all the key government figures and allowed them to speak to the media freely. The Prime Minister and several other ministers went live, addressing people via televised broadcasts during the coup. However, it is a well-known fact that in the past, coup plotters would normally arrest all important figures with no one allowed to speak to the media. Not going after the government members and allowing them to freely speak to different media outlets also raises a lot of questions.

Furthermore, F-16s flying over Istanbul did not prevent Erdogan's passenger plane from landing, even though it was clear that if he successfully landed, the coup attempt would be over. The pro-Erdogan media argued after the fact that Erdogan's Gulfstream G450 type TC-ATA small passenger airplane could not be stopped by the F-16's because it was presented as a passenger plane tagged THY 8456 before it landed[15]. However, at the same time Erdogan's plane's coordinates were being broadcast in social media with its exact coordinates and even its position on maps was being constantly updated by different Twitter accounts and in other social media platforms[16]. Furthermore, it would be naïve to believe that serious coup attempters would not be able to track down Erdogan's plane's position with the military technologies they had in their hands while the plane's coordinates were being spread all over the social media anyways.

Also the Parliament building was attacked by the F-16s in Ankara in a strange move that does not have anything to do with a coup and it is still unclear the rationale behind these attacks—unless it was to create a strong sense of nationalism, outrage and unity among the general population to rally behind President Erdogan who flew into Istanbul on cue, to call for just such demonstrations and outpourings of loyalty and outrage. Several Parliamentarians rushed to the Parliament buildings according to the narratives in the media as they learned of the coup attempt in an effort to counter it. During that time F-16s dropped around ten bombs on the Parliamentary buildings and a helicopter that was over powered by the security forces on the scene tried to land at the National Assembly's garden. The coup plotters again failed to utilize the full forces at their disposal, including land forces around the Parliament and allowed Parliamentarians to freely gather to counter the coup attempt by a joint statement[17]. If the coup makers were really serious about interrupting any progress in the Parliament building, they needed to use a squadron of soldiers to surround and empty the Parliament building, not to bombing it. It is a common sense that bombing the National Assembly would critically diminish any support that would be extended to the coup and would turn people away from it.

Indeed, senior AKP leadership and their representatives in the media called people to the streets for mass demonstrations, a move the coup plotters evidently failed to see and calculate. It is obvious that coup plotters risk all and plan ahead their actions and strategies for success. All precautions and

---

[14] "A Group of Soldiers Enters CNN-Turk Building" http://www.cnnturk.com/turkiye/asker-cnn-turk-binasina-girdi
[15] "How Erdogan's Plane Deceives F-16s" http://www.cnnturk.com/turkiye/cumhurbaskani-erdoganin-ucagi-darbecilerin-f16larini-atlatarak-alana-indi
[16] "A Website Close to the CIA Made Erdogan's Plane an Open Target" https://www.sadecehaber.com/cia-sitesi-darbe-gecesi-erdoganin-ucagini-acik-hedef-yapti
[17] "Parliament Deputies Talk about the Last Night: We have Questions?" http://www.birgun.net/haber-detay/milletvekilleri-dun-geceyi-anlatiyor-sorulacak-sorular-var-120221.html

measures are calculated in a way to lead to success. However, with the July 15 coup attempt, it is clear that the planners of this coup did not want to be successful or had somehow been undercut from their first moves.

The existence of inconsistent accounts of Erdogan and his close circles about the coup have also caused more uncertainties and reservations about the coup attempt. For example, Erdogan himself stated five different time frames to account when and how he learned about the coup attempt[18].

If we continue to analyze the aftermath of the coup, we can find many more inconsistencies. For example, Erdogan connected to a TV station via facetime calling people to the streets to support him. At the same time almost without knowing anything about the coup makers and who were behind the coup, Erdogan blamed Mr. Gulen, a Turkish self-exiled Muslim cleric in Pennsylvania, for being behind the coup. That blame continued as he made his speech at the Ataturk airport. It was not clear how Erdogan gathered the evidence and knowledge about who was behind the coup attempt while running away from the coup makers. Later, however cell phone traffic, text-messaging and email intercepts by the UK GCHQ among Erdogan's high government officials were leaked in the German press (Focus magazine[19]) showing them agreeing even in the first moments of the coup to blame Gulen for it[20].

Erdogan Lands at Ataturk Airport as the Hero

As Erdogan landed at Ataturk airport, he was greeted with thousands of his supporters. It was clear that the coup attempt was over in a few hours and Erdogan all of a sudden became a hero and savior of democracy, versus its clear and longstanding enemy.

Immediately after Erdogan left Ataturk airport, in two to three hours, a list of 1563 military officers suddenly appeared in which those listed were blamed as the organizers and participators of the coup attempt. The prepared list supposedly involved the active coup participating military personnel, but most of the officers in the list were not directly or indirectly involved with the coup, nor could such a list have been so quickly prepared after the coup. It very clearly had been prepared ahead of time.

If one were to believe Erdogan's government, strangely enough, while the mass demonstrations and post-coup attempt precautions were going on, the security and intelligence forces in an extremely short time period investigated the coup, analyzed and figured out who was behind it and found out the coup makers, compiling a list of 1563 officers from all around the country, including listing their whereabouts, their present addresses and got warrants on all of them signed by prosecutors, had judges approve the warrants and distributed that list to eighty-one different provinces all over Turkey so that the perpetrators of the coup could be arrested. I was head of the Turkish National Police Counter Terrorism Unit and I can tell you that from a policing and judiciary standpoint, this is simply impossible.

---

[18] *"When Erdogan Learned about the Coup Attempt. Inconsistencies of Time Frames at Erdogan's Accounts"* http://www.cumhuriyet.com.tr/foto/foto_galeri/575077/1/Darbe_girisimini_ne_zaman_ogrendi__Erdogan_in_soz lerindeki_saat_farkliliklari.html

[19] *"Report: British Intel Proves Erdogan Staged the Turkey Coup, "Will Blame Gulen's Hizmet, Sack Millions""* http://www.thedailysheeple.com/report-british-intel-proves-erdogan-staged-the-turkey-coup-will-blame-gulens-hizmet-sack-millions_072016

[20] *"German Focus: Tomorrow the Purge Begins, We Accuse Gulenists"* http://romanyahaber.com/2016/07/24/focus-dergisi-ingilizler-ipucu-yakaladi-dedi/

All those post-coup investigations and operational activities somehow magically were carried out in less than three hours and massive arrests started around the country which targeted not only the officers who were involved in the coup attempt but also several other hundreds who did not have anything to do with it. Many were arrested during their vacations at resorts or at their homes. Some of the generals who were arrested were also clearly against the coup attempt and did not allow their personnel to get involved as they stood by the government. However, that reality was not enough to save them and somehow their names were in the list.

I worked for counterterrorism and operations divisions of the Turkish National Police for my entire tenure with the police as a mid-level manager and later as the Chief of Police in Ankara and Sanliurfa. I have been involved in hundreds of operations and I clearly know the capacity of the police in investigations and operations. Under normal circumstances the highest number the police would consider for a mass operation would be fifty and that would only be possible in the major cities. For an operation of fifty targets, the police would work at least six months prior to the operation to prepare the paperwork, investigation and evidence files against the suspects. Making a list of fifty suspects with their present addresses would even take at least a day or two to ensure there would not be any mistakes in the addresses raided with armed operations. Preparing a major list of 1563 military officers in just under three hours all with their addresses and whereabouts all over Turkey is simply impossible. Gathering such a list with exact present addresses would take days, if not weeks, apart from any investigative activities. Therefore, it is very clear that the arrestee list was prepared well before the coup and also the officers who were going to be arrested were distinguished in advance regardless of their role in the actual coup attempt.

Furthermore, as the first day passed, the arrests did not stop and it was clear and obvious that a very decisive and quick operational groundwork was already in place. People who had nothing to do with the coup attempt, or even did not have any ties with the military or coup makers were unceasingly and mercilessly arrested.

The government started to arrest and fire officers from different elements of society including teachers, doctors, university professors, judges, prosecutors, police officers, people working for different ministries, religious affairs and even workers including drivers and low skilled job employees immediately—all of whom are slowly being replaced with Erdogan's own loyal subjects. Especially the Hizmet movement and people close to Mr. Gulen were targeted. However, a wide range of society from different elements of the public were also arrested and soon people realized that the purge and arrests were not about only the Gulen movement—anyone who opposed Erdogan regardless of his/her ideology were victims of this new wave of arrests and firings. Eventually, the total number of the purged and fired officers from different government posts exceeded 100,000 and the people who were arrested or detained surpassed over 60,000[21]. Some of them have been tortured, others like a nursing mother and wife of a police officer, and an elderly mother of a journalist were arrested in lieu of the actual person under investigation—held until he turned himself in.

One of the prosecutors who was on the list of fired prosecutors and judges, actually had died from natural causes 57 days prior to the coup attempt. In fact, according to journalist Saygi Ozturk the list that contained names of 2075 fired prosecutors and judges was prepared two years ago based on in

---

[21]*"Turkey widens post-coup purge"* http://turkeypurge.com/

which cities they were working at the time[22]. This alone proves that the lists were arranged before the coup.

Following the coup, some of Parliament members pushed a bill to establish an investigation commission, a constitutional tool to investigate critical incidents occurring in the country. However, Erdogan was against it and ordered his AKP party not to accept this petition which was then overturned with AKP votes. If Erdogan and AKP were so sure of themselves about the coup attempt, why wouldn't they accept a Parliamentary investigation to uncover the details of the coup also raises another challenging question.

The coup attempt was carried out by a group of military officers whom named themselves Yurtta Sulh Cuntasi, or Peace at Home Junta. However, to this day nobody knows the members of the junta, who assumed what kind of role and what were the ranks of the officers in it. If the junta had led the coup, not revealing the identities of the junta members still is one of the biggest and most important mysteries of this coup attempt. So far nobody knows who were the leaders of the coup attempt and who were the members of the junta.

The official criminal investigations during the court proceedings are being carried out secretly based on the decision of the courts. Because of that no one has seen any evidence against the arrested coup attempters and the public is not informed about the statements of military officers. The only statements made public are the statements which are leaked to pro-Erdogan newspapers and belong to the arrestees seen on TV and in newspapers confessing, after they were tortured. Therefore, if the government is not hiding anything, they would not carry out the investigations clandestinely and would reveal all the details of the coup attempt they uncovered during their investigations to the public without any hesitations. Likewise, the use of torture makes any confession suspicious.

The physical evidence that we can learn so far from the media through the purposefully leaked details of the investigations do not shed any light over the coup attempt. The biggest physical evidence put before of the public was one dollar bills which were said to be a signal and identifier of those involved with Gulen and the coup. For days the media close to Erdogan published the pictures of dollar bills that were found in the possession of arrested military personnel. For example, Diyarbakir Army corps commander Lieutenant General Ibrahim Yilmaz was arrested because he had a one-dollar bill in his possession even though himself and his officers were not involved in the coup attempt. When asked by the media as he was arrested, Lieutenant General Yilmaz explained that he often traveled overseas as part of his duty and he had in his wallet a one-hundred-dollar bill, a five-dollar-bill and two one-dollar-bills at the time of his arrest. He added that he also had Euros and Franks at his home simply because he traveled abroad frequently[23]. However, he was arrested anyway. Like him, hundreds were arrested because of one dollar bills, an act of craziness as several people in Turkey used to distribute one dollar bills during wedding ceremonies as gestures. Another evidence put in front of the public came out to be a GTA (grand theft auto) video game cheat sheet.

---

[22] "A Prosecutor Fired for being Coup Supporter Actually Had Died 2 Months Ago"
http://www.baroturk.com/hsyknin-darbe-girisimine-iliskin-aciga-aldigi-savcilardan-biri-2-ay-once-olmus-23371h.htm
[23] "Diyarbakir Army corps commander Lieutenant General Ibrahim Yilmaz: 'I am Innocent'"
http://www.hedefhalk.com/tutuklanan-diyarbakir-7nci-kolordu-komutani-ibrahim-yilmaz-ben-masumum-817488h.htm

It is claimed in the media that a team of SAT commandos were sent during the coup to arrest Erdogan in Marmaris where he was taking his vacation for the last week. Extraordinarily, the commando team sent to arrest Erdogan could not find the address where he was staying and asked people on the streets where his hotel was[24]. If Erdogan was the prime target of the coup, how could the team sent to arrest him have not planned their operation in depth beforehand? What kind of professional operation team going after such a high important target arrives to the scene in such an absurd way to not to know the address of their prime target remains to this day, a mystery as well.

Turkish Military Chief of Staff, Hulusi Akar's accounts for the coup are also inconsistent. According to Turkish National Intelligence (TNI), Akar was informed about the coup around 4 p.m. by the Director of the TNI Fidan personally going to the Chief of Staff's headquarters. However, Akar had not informed anyone including the President and the Prime Minister about the coup attempt based on the statements. The Prime Minister stated in public that he first learned about the coup around 9 p.m. when President Erdogan called him and added that he could not reach to the Chief of Staff when he tried to call him at 9 pm. President Erdogan on his account provided several different time frames ranging from 4 pm to 9 pm and obviously Akar was not among the people who informed him of the coup. Furthermore, even though Akar was informed about the coup attempt, he did not order for any preparations nor did he carry out any activity to halt or to prevent the coup attempt while he was sitting in his office without any extra security measures against the coup, even though it is very obvious that the Chief of Staff himself would be one of the prime targets of coup makers. Furthermore, Akar did not communicate with the Chief Commander of the Air Force who was in a wedding in Istanbul and the Chief Commander of the Gendarmerie who was also in a wedding in Ankara both of whom claimed that they learned about the coup from television while they were at wedding ceremonies[25]. Akar also claimed that the coup plotters put a gun on his head to sign the coup statement in the middle of the coup[26]. However, it does not make any sense for the coup attempters to worry about the legality of their actions as they are by default illegal till they seize the power, and if they can't seize the power no amount of paperwork is going to save them nevertheless. All these accounts are highly suspicious and clearly indicate the existence of a pre-arranged and staged coup attack. Under normal circumstances, a commander of the military would do everything in his power to halt and prevent a coup attempt and would communicate with his top brass immediately. However, we obviously see that clearly he was not concerned at all. More abnormally Akar and some of his top aides were not fired after the coup even though they did not take any measures to stop it.

Finally, Major General Mehmet Disli who is the brother of AKP Deputy Chairman Saban Disli[27] was told to be one of the main organizers of the coup attempt. General Disli was among the coup makers who forced Chief of Staff Hulusi Akar to sign the coup statement by putting a gun on his head and by strangling him with a belt based on Akar's statement. Akar with other arrested generals were sent to Akinci base as captives. However, strangely Disli accompanied Akar after he was saved from Akinci base as the coup was over. It is extremely difficult to understand why Akar would let someone to accompany

[24] "SAT Commandos Asked People on the Streets about Whereabouts of Erdogan"
http://www.timeturk.com/cumhurbaskani-erdogan-in-yerini-sivillere-sormuslar/haber-215614
[25] "An Army of Inconsistencies" http://www.cumhuriyet.com.tr/haber/turkiye/574782/Bir_ordu_celiski.html
[26] "They Put a Gun on Akar's Head and his Throat was Tied with a Belt" http://www.hurriyet.com.tr/genelkurmay-baskani-hulusi-akarin-basina-silah-dayadilar-bogazini-kemerle-siktilar-40150883
[27] https://www.akparti.org.tr/english/yonetim/baskanliklar

him after his release as the coup attempt was over; especially someone who threatened to kill him hours ago[28]. If Disli was among the coup makers, why he was with Akar when they went to Prime Ministry building on July 16 morning remains one of the greatest uncertainties of the coup attempt.

Furthermore, over eight thousand military officers were arrested and almost ninety percent of them were not involved with the coup directly. They were either arrested at their homes or at vacation places. So far nobody knows what was the relationship of the arrested officers with the coup makers. Half of the generals in the Turkish military, over one hundred-forty, and about six hundred colonels were arrested. Several other officers from the military were also fired[29]. If over half of the high-level military officers were involved in the coup somehow based on the arrests and the purge, why they were not successful and risked their futures in failing is also unclear.

Conclusions

The existence of unanswered inquirers and inconsistent accounts of Erdogan and his close circles have caused more uncertainties and reservations about the coup attempt rather than clarify what really happened.

Surprisingly, a clear pre-Coup pivot to reviving relations with Putin's Russia and also Israel occurred as Erdogan realized that the Zarrab case in federal court likely number's his days of any type of salvageable relationship with the U.S. Floundering to stay in power and to consolidate that power, Erdogan has now become a totalitarian dictator and is in the process of setting up a vertical system of governance much like Putin's. Indeed, the military generals who survived the coup are pro-Russian[30], where as those that were fired were pro-Western, a harm that U.S. Central Command Commander Gen. Joseph Votel said would be a loss to collaborative efforts with the West[31]. Erdogan also has accepted a pledge of 500 billion dollars[32] from Saudi Arabia to keep him in power. Likewise, he continues to illicitly and even openly support ISIS who help him to keep the Kurdish issue at bay.

Furthermore, the worst is not only the arrests that took place. Amnesty International reports that military officers arrested in Ankara and Istanbul were bloodied and even raped to exhort confessions from them[33]. Youth were arrested without reasons. Anyone carrying a dollar bill, even wedding revelers throwing dollar bills to the newly wedded couple were arrested and charged as terrorists. Anti-American sentiment was fanned into flames with the Incirlik air base surrounded by demonstrators as Erdogan's

---

[28] *"Major General Mehmet Disli Puzzlement"* http://www.sozcu.com.tr/2016/gundem/mehmet-disli-muammasi-1319328/

[29] *"Several Generals are Detained"* http://www.sozcu.com.tr/2016/gundem/cok-sayida-general-ve-amiral-gozaltinda-il-il-gozalti-listesi-1317450/

[30] *"Playing with Fire: Erdogan's Anti-U.S. Scheme"* By Ahmet S Yayla & Anne Speckhard
http://www.worldpolicy.org/blog/2016/07/27/playing-fire-erdo%C4%9Fans-anti-us-scheme

[31] *"Pentagon Allies Jailed in Turkey Amid Coup Backlash, General Says"*
http://blogs.wsj.com/washwire/2016/07/28/pentagon-allies-jailed-in-turkey-amid-coup-backlash-general-says/

[32] *"King Salman Decides to Invest 500 billion dollars in Turkey"* https://www.sadecehaber.com/kral-selmandan-turkiyeye-550-milyar-dolarlik-yatirim

[33] *"Turkey detainees tortured, raped after failed coup, rights group says"*
http://www.cnn.com/2016/07/26/europe/turkey-coup-attempt-aftermath/

controlled press whipped them into a frenzy of believing the Americans were behind the coup and unbelievably, were harboring ISIS members at the base[34].

Western policy makers need to formulate the right combination of incentives and disincentives to deal with Erdogan. Obviously, Erdogan is no longer a friend of the U.S. and its NATO allies, and likely can never be so again. While the world clearly needs Turkey to stem the flow of foreign fighters and now those leaving ISIS—as they will likely be dangerous to the EU, Balkans and to U.S. interests at home and abroad, it is unlikely the democratic West can offer anything to Erdogan—except support as a totalitarian dictator and immunity from corruption charges—that would entice him to meet the West's needs in the fight against ISIS and the struggle to bring peace in Syria and Iraq. Erdogan has not been a true ally to the U.S. and to the West for years now—shutting down the free press and supporting terrorist organizations on their soil and in Syria and Iraq. He will not be the West's ally in the future for sure. And Russia's Putin is delighted to use him as a member of NATO with full veto power and to embrace him as the totalitarian dictator that he has become—arresting, torturing, imprisoning and purging any that oppose him.

We need to stand strong and firm as a supporter of democratic Turkey with freedom of expression, human rights and the free press which is essential in all democracies. We also need to stand against torture and a radically unjust judicial system. Turkey is clearly being governed by an oppressive regime now. The due process, rule of law, human rights and simply human dignity mean nothing for this regime as long as its illicit objectives can be met. Erdogan and his close circles for years have now gotten away with crushing the press, massive corruption and illicit dealings, human rights violations and the open and hidden support provided to terrorist organizations in the region including ISIS. With the press under government control, ordinary Turkish citizens have no access to the truth and they cannot really understand what is going on in Turkey. Undoubtedly, Western policy makers must understand that there is an urgent need to formulate effective responses to deal with this oppressive regime which is now blackmailing the United States with the Incirlik air base and the fight against ISIS and the EU with the open flow of Syrian refugees. Otherwise, very soon, we will have to deal with a new Turkey and a possibly even a new Political Islamist Turkish Dictatorship—a country that may become the Sunni version of Iran, as we watch Turkey cut its ties with the West and NATO and approach even closer to Russia and to radical and extremists elements in the Middle East.

Ahmet S. Yayla, Ph.D. is co-author of the just released book, *ISIS Defectors: Inside Stories of the Terrorist Caliphate.* He is Deputy Director of the International Center for the Study of Violent Extremism (ICSVE) and is also Adjunct Professor of Criminology, Law and Society at George Mason University. He formerly served as Professor and the Chair of the Sociology Department at Harran University in Turkey. He is the former Chief of Counterterrorism and Operations Division for the Turkish National Police with a 20-year career interviewing terrorists.

---

[34] *"Cuppeli Ahmet Analyses Post Coup Attempt and Calls People to Prayers"* http://akmusluman.com/cubbeli-ahmet-hoca-efendi-gundemi-degerlendirerek-vatandaslara-onemli-bir-cagrid/

Mr. ROHRABACHER. Well, thank you. And we will keep your son in mind. And——

Mr. YAYLA. Thank you.

Mr. ROHRABACHER [continuing]. I hope whoever is reading this testimony in Turkey understands that we know who your son is, and we will not—it will not escape our attention if he is continued in captivity.

Dr. Stein, would you like to proceed?

STATEMENT OF AARON STEIN, PH.D., RESIDENT SENIOR FELLOW, RAFIK HARIRI CENTER FOR THE MIDDLE EAST, ATLANTIC COUNCIL

Mr. STEIN. Thank you very much. Thank you, Mr. Chairman, other members of the committee, as well as my panelists for the opportunity to speak today.

I am going to dispense with reading my full statement, and instead, in the interest of time, just focus on the main takeaways.

I think the failed coup on July 15, I mean, it was obviously a very serious event, and I think the scale of the Turkish trauma has been underestimated in this country, even people who say that they understand that this was a serious event I think still to a certain extent underestimate what took place on July 15.

I also believe that the coup plotters themselves have been cast wrong. You know, I don't think that they were these series of bumbling fools who made a series of errors. I think that they were very serious individuals. I think the coup attempt was larger than most people realized. It involved a number of different branches of the armed services from two different land—you know, land armies, the air force special operations command, the navy, and the coast guard. And I do think that there is, you know, enough evidence put forward in the Turkish press to say that there was Gulenist involvement, but there were also a lot of other people involved as well.

The post-coup purges have obviously been very, very large. I believe the last count was 80,000 suspended, with some tens of thousands formally arrested. I think it is important to note that a lot of these purges have public support in Turkey, and that is because of the deep distrust amongst various elements of the Turkish, you know, both electorate and people for Fethullah Gulen and his role in Turkish society. But I will say this: I think there are signs that this unity and this general support for the purges is beginning to pass. So, if the rally around the flag, you know, is always palpable in states or countries that undergo trauma, you know, thinking about our own country after 9/11, it eventually does pass, and I think we are in that moment at the moment in Turkey.

I do believe, however, that the sense of nationalism has been bolstered by two interrelated things. One is that there is a concurrent war going—or counterinsurgency, I should call it, in the southeast between the Turkish security forces and the PKK. And just to give a sense of how large that conflict is—it largely escapes international attention—is, since July, there has been greater than 600 Turkish security personnel killed and, in a number of different cities that have been destroyed by fighting, more than 500,000 IDPs. So this is independent of the Syria conflict as well.

And the other is the instrumentalization of anti-Americanism. Now, I agree with Mr. Makovsky that this has been instrumentalized and that this is largely a populist crutch that the Turkish Government is using, one, because I believe, as, you know, a public opinion poll has pointed out, that people do actually believe that the United States was involved in the coup. I think that is far more widespread than most people realize. And if we weren't directly involved, because, you know, trying to explain the ins and outs of extradition law to any public, you know, causes most people's eyes to glaze over and they flip the channel.

And the other is that it is useful because it is always easier to blame the foreign other than it is to look internally to what was a very domestic Turkish event that the United States has nothing to do with the coup; we have nothing to do with the execution of Turkish domestic politics, with one exception, that Fethullah Gulen is a green card holder.

The Turkish military, I will focus on as I begin to wrap up, has already been affected, and the operational readiness is nowhere near where it was before the coup began: 149 flag-ranking officers have been purged, replaced with 99, so they are 50 short of admirals and generals than where we were on July 14. The air force has plans to shutter three squadrons, perhaps in addition to two more, for a total of five, which means that the operational readiness with the commitments that they have in three different countries, their own, Iraq, and Syria, you know, begin to come into question about how large a scale and how they can actually sustain current level of operations both against ISIS and the PKK.

And I think, in closing, I think it is important for us all to realize that Turkey is actually unstable, and it is a very difficult ally, but nevertheless, it is an important ally. I mean, you can't really put your finger on anything that says, "This is why Turkey is absolutely instrumental for American interests abroad," except for the idea that NATO matters, transatlantic relations matter, especially at a time when that sort of fundamental aspect of American foreign policy is being called into question more and more about the value of overseas alliance.

Thank you very much.

[The prepared statement of Mr. Stein follows:]

Dr. Aaron Stein

Senior Fellow, Atlantic Council's Rafik Hariri Center for the Middle East

"Turkey After the July Coup Attempt," House Committee on Foreign Affairs, Subcommittee on Europe, Asia, and Emerging Threats

September 14, 2016

The failed coup attempt in Turkey has had a profound effect on Turkish society and bureaucratic institutions. As the coup attempt was unfolding, the Turkish government blamed Fetullah Gulen, a cleric from Turkey's Nur movement, for instructing his followers in the military and bureaucracy to overthrow Turkey's democratically government.

The events of July 15th are still, largely, a mystery. The evidence available in open sources does suggest that Gulenists played a part in the coup attempt, but it also appears that Kemalists and Turkish nationalists were also involved. Contrary to the narrative, the coup plotters were not bumbling fools. The putchists included officers from different branches of the Turkish military, including: the Air Force, the land forces (with representation from two different armies, the first and second), special operations forces (Maroon Berets), and the Navy and Coast Guard. The plotters nearly succeeded in their primary mission, the decapitation of government, but also appear to have been operating under the false assumption that the Turkish people would accept military rule. The latter assumption proved inaccurate and, ultimately, the start of protests against the putchists' actions upended the coup attempt.

In the weeks following the failed coup attempt, the Turkish public has "rallied around the flag" and lent support to measures taken to purge Gulenists from state institutions. To date, more than 80,000 public servants have been suspended from work, with many of them arrested for alleged Gulenist ties. Fetullah Gulen has little popular support and Turkey and these purges are viewed as long overdue and necessary for the long-term health of Turkish bureaucratic institutions.

Nationalist sentiment in Turkey has increased following the coup attempt, with many Turks blaming the United States and the European Union for failing to show proper solidarity with their NATO ally. The AKP has instrumentalized this growing anti-Western sentiment for two reasons: First, there are elements within the AKP and, certainly, among its voter base that genuinely believe that the United States was involved in the coup, or at the very least, was hedging its bets during the coup attempt because of concerns about Erdogan and political Islam. Second, the blaming of the "foreign other" helps to absolve the AKP of its own role in helping to grow the Gulenist presence in the Turkish bureaucracy – and by extension, how its own efforts to coup proof the military contributed to the July 15th coup attempt.

The United States – obviously – had nothing to do with the coup attempt in Turkey, nor was the White House slow to condemn the events of July 15th. The coup attempt and subsequent purges are entirely a result of Turkish domestic politics and political culture that has nothing to do with the United States, with one exception: Gulen is a U.S. green card holder.

Fetullah Gulen fled Turkey for the United States in 1999, following the so-called "post-modern coup," wherein the Turkish military used the threat of a military intervention to force the government to resign. Following the post-modern coup, Turkish authorities banned the Welfare Party and its leader,

Necmettin Erbakan, from politics. Erbakan is the father of Turkey's political Islamist movement and mentor of the current Turkish President, Recep Tayyip Erdogan.

The Turkish military and elements of the bureaucracy accused Gulen of instructing his followers to infiltrate the bureaucracy and military, in order to eventually remake the Turkish state – the very same charges that the Turkish government is currently accusing him of.

Gulen and AKP forged an alliance following these events, deepening their partnership after the 2002 election. The AKP relied heavily on the Gulenists for more than a decade, largely to increase the number of "friendly" elements in the Turkish bureaucracy and military. The two groups were symbiotic, in that the AKP needed the Gulenists to act as a political counterweight to Kemalist elements in the Turkish bureaucracy and the military, while Gulenists relied on the AKP to grow in strength.

In the case of the latter, the AKP gave political and bureaucratic support to Gulenist-led trials – Ergenekon and Balyoz – that accused members of the military of plotting a coup. These trials resulted in the suspensions and arrest of numerous high ranking officers. Many of the officers promoted to take their place have since been accused of sympathizing with the July 15th coup and have been discharged from the Turkish military.

The military purges have had a serious impact on Turkish military readiness and capabilities. A total of 149 Admirals and Generals were purged after the failed coup, which prompted the Turkish government to promote 99 officers to take their place. Currently, Turkey has some 50 less flag-ranking-officers than before the coup. The Air Force has also suffered. 274 Air Force pilots have been discharged and Turkey now faces a serious fighter pilot shortage, with the number of F-16 pilots dropping from a healthy 1.25:1 pilot-to-cockpit ratio to just .8:1. In response, Turkey has shuttered three F-16 squadrons and has plans to shutter two more. This shortage comes amid Turkey's continuing air operations in support of its counterinsurgent campaign in southeastern Turkey and Iraqi Kurdistan, alongside the commitments made to cross border operations in Syria, as part of Operation Euphrates Shield. This shortage could impact Turkish military planning in the near term, a reality that the United States should account for when considering potential collaboration with the Turkish Armed Forces in Syria, or for NATO operations in a different, unforeseen, contingency.

The tempo of operations for airstrikes against the PKK does appear to have slowed in recent weeks, perhaps because finite assets are now being asked to protect ground forces in Syria. This comes amid continuing unrest in Turkey's southeast and near-daily PKK attacks on military and civilian targets. In this latest round of fighting, 676 Turkish security force members have been killed in attacks, with the plurality dying in improvised explosive attacks since July 2015. Numerous Kurdish-majority cities have also been destroyed and there are now more than 400, 000 internally displaced people, independent of the refugee burden posed by the Syrian civil conflict. In recent days, the Turkish government has replaced 28 elected mayors, the majority of which were Kurds from the Democratic Peoples' Party, or HDP. The HDP's leadership, Selahattin Demirtas and Figen Yuksedag, both of whom are under investigation and face lengthy prison sentences, have called for street protests.

In the near term, Turkey will remain unstable. The purges have impacted every key Turkish institution and will have an impact on governance and security. The Turkish Air Force is suffering from a pilot shortage and the military is being asked to fight a two-front counterinsurgent war in three different countries: Turkey, Syria, and Iraq. Turkish domestic politics remains fractured along ethnic and nationalist fault lines, with the Kurdish issue being the most pronounced, amid a façade of political unity after the failed coup attempt. These issues are local to Turkey and have little to do with the United States, other than Washington's interest in a stable Turkey, capable of pulling its weight in the NATO alliance. In the near term, the United States should prepare for a period of tension with Ankara. These tensions are linked to Gulen's status in the United States, the concurrent Department of Justice-led review of Turkey's extradition request, and divergences over Syria policy. In the longer term, however, both sides have an incentive to look beyond these disagreements. Turkey is a NATO ally and is part of the 60 or so countries with which the United States has a military alliance or partnership. The U.S. has an interest in preserving these partnerships because its interests are global and require strong relationships with countries in key global regions.

Mr. ROHRABACHER. That last statement was——

Mr. WEBER. Interesting.

Mr. ROHRABACHER [continuing]. Is very important, in that we have to—look, Turkey—I am 69 years old, for those younger people out there who haven't been around that long. Ever since I can remember, the Turks have always been at our side, and we have been at their side. What a tragedy to lose that goodwill and that sense of family that we have had with the Turks. And that is one of the reasons why as, over the years, there have been different controversies and areas of friction that have emerged, I have always bent over backwards to try to be fair to my Turkish friends, because they are our friends.

And, unfortunately, we have now, from what I can see, is that the government has gone—the Government of Turkey has gone way beyond its bounds of not only propriety but of any type of acceptable response to what was an illegal and bloody and thuggish, as I say, coup attempt. And a thuggish coup attempt does not justify creating a dictatorship and an oppressive regime allied with radical Islamic forces and eliminating pro-Western people from areas of influence in their country. There is no justification for it, although we have to recognize, as all of our folks have, that they have gone through a trauma.

However, that is where my line of questioning begins, I would suggest, I believe, that just what you can presume that this didn't just happen in terms of the response. This was not a response to something that happened. That response was in place. In other words, there—and I will ask Mr. Yayla about this. You said that, within a matter of hours, thousands of people were being arrested. What does that indicate to you as a former officer in Turkish intelligence and law enforcement, that those arrests were ready to be made even before the coup? Isn't that correct?

Mr. YAYLA. Definitely. You cannot make just a list of 1,653 people from the military as the police—or as the intelligence, because the lists are not out there. So those lists were studied, analyzed, investigated at least, in my experience, 6 months before. And in hours, very short term, while you are dealing with the trauma, with all your forces in the field fighting against the coup makers, with your intelligence and investigators on the—taking precautions and preventative measures, you cannot prepare a list of 1,653 military officers and most of whom were not directly involved with the coup, also. Several of them were taken from their vacation places. And there was not any indication that those people were related with the coup.

Mr. ROHRABACHER. So we have all kinds of people who had nothing to do with the coup——

Mr. YAYLA. No.

Mr. ROHRABACHER [continuing]. Who have been arrested, and we have, obviously, a list of people to be arrested long before the coup even happened.

Mr. YAYLA. Yes. In the list, there were deceased people. There were several people wrongly listed, and they were already fired. Even though they were fired, they were relisted. So it also shows that the lists were prearranged because they refired five people.

Mr. ROHRABACHER. Right. I would like to ask our first two witnesses to put this in perspective for us. Was there this type—was there a major increase, because last time we had a hearing, that is one of the things we talked about, an increase of repression going on in Turkey before the coup? Did we see journalists arrested? Did we see newspapers closed? Did we see opposition parties or whatever suppressed before the coup?

Ms. OGNIANOVA. I can speak about the situation with the press and the media. We have been following daily events, press freedom events in Turkey for years, but because of the magnitude of the crackdown, which had started months and months before the coup attempt, we were compelled to create a daily chronicle of those events. We started putting it out in March, which is when the—we thought that was the peak of repressions, when the Zaman—the Feza media group, which includes Zaman and a number of other big pro-Gulen media, were basically confiscated by the state.

Mr. ROHRABACHER. And that is—when was that?

Ms. OGNIANOVA. That was in March. And that was really a peak moment that we thought that this was the culmination of months and months before that of repressions, but we were wrong because after we started this daily chronicle in March, we started reporting and documenting dozens of cases on a weekly basis.

Mr. ROHRABACHER. Dozens of cases——

Ms. OGNIANOVA. Dozens of cases of violations of press freedom, including detentions of journalists, prosecutions on politically motivated charges, including terrorism charges, criminal charges, insult charges, the de facto imprisonment of detained journalists, the shuttering of media outlets——

Mr. ROHRABACHER. Okay.

Ms. OGNIANOVA [continuing]. Their confiscation by the government and their use for—basically they became mouthpieces.

Mr. ROHRABACHER. Okay. Thank you. We see, in the press area, there was this repression a long time before the coup.

Ms. OGNIANOVA. A long time before the coup.

Mr. ROHRABACHER. So no matter how thuggish the coup was, that can't be an excuse for the tyranny that happened even before it and, as we heard from the witness, was probably arranged—the thousands of people were probably arranged even before there was a coup.

Mr. Makovsky what about—excuse me. The press, what about other opposition parties, et cetera, did we have that type of repression before the coup?

Mr. MAKOVKSY. Yeah. Absolutely. I would fully associate myself with Ms. Ognianova's remarks. And as I testified last time, media repression in Turkey has been going on for years, and a lot of it has been very insidious and not so visible: In-house censorship, a lot of self-censorship, many firings have been going on for a long time. Most people who work on Turkey in this town have many friends who suffered as a result, journalist friends and—suffered well long before the coup.

I wonder, Mr. Chairman, if it is the appropriate time, I was going to say a word or two about the Gulen movement and the——

Mr. ROHRABACHER. You know what? Let's hold that off until the other questions——

Mr. MAKOVKSY. Sure.

Mr. ROHRABACHER [continuing]. But I will suggest, unless one of my colleagues would like to ask specifically about it, but if it does not get covered in the questions, we will come back, and I will be asking all of you what specifically you believe about the Gulenist movement. Is it indeed a conspiratorial movement that tries to in some way capture power from a democratically elected government?

And do you have one comment on whether or not this repression that came immediately after the coup and what we have been talking about was in some way already in place before the coup?

Mr. STEIN. I would agree with most of the statements from the colleagues. Yes, because it was in place of when the Gulen movement and the AKP had their political falling out in December 2013, so I would say beginning in January 2014 was when you had what we would call purges beginning. And so, yes, those lists were already there, because the targeting of the Gulen movement and its listing as a terrorist organization in Turkey had already taken place before that.

Mr. ROHRABACHER. Right. And correct me if I am wrong. The falling out—that the Gulenist movement supported Erdogan prior to—well, when he was first coming to power politically, and the falling out they had was after the Gulenists in the media reported on corruption of the Erdogan government. Is that correct?

Ms. OGNIANOVA. If I can just——

Mr. ROHRABACHER. Right. That is when—okay. Jump in at that point, and then we will go on to my colleagues.

Ms. OGNIANOVA. There were released recordings of conversations, or alleged conversations, between government officials, including Erdogan, and his family members and other members of his——

Mr. ROHRABACHER. Right.

Ms. OGNIANOVA [continuing]. Circle that were leaked on social media first, and from there on, the media picked them up.

Mr. ROHRABACHER. But the——

Ms. OGNIANOVA. So they were first leaked on——

Mr. ROHRABACHER. But the actual——

Ms. OGNIANOVA [continuing]. The media——

Mr. ROHRABACHER. But the actual——

Ms. OGNIANOVA [continuing]. On social media.

Mr. ROHRABACHER. The releases were releases concerning——

Ms. OGNIANOVA. Corruption.

Mr. ROHRABACHER [continuing]. Corruption. Right.

Ms. OGNIANOVA. Correct.

Mr. ROHRABACHER. That is an——

Ms. OGNIANOVA. Correct.

Mr. ROHRABACHER [continuing]. Important distinction between somebody who gets mad because his children are being talked about in a bad way on social media versus somebody who is angry because his corrupt practices that were enriching him and his family have been exposed. It is a big difference.

It is yours. Mr. Meeks.

Mr. MEEKS. Thank you, Mr. Chairman.

As I indicated in my opening statement, you know, I am always concerned about democracy and democratic institutions. So my first question would be, were any members of the Parliament allegedly a part of the coup d'etat? Does anybody know? From any parties. Were any arrested or charged with anything or dismissed from the Parliament or anything of that nature?

Mr. MAKOVKSY. There were charges against some of the Kurdish members of the Parliament, but not specifically about the coup.

Mr. MEEKS. Right. I am talking about the coup. I am talking specifically about the coup at this point.

Mr. MAKOVKSY. Not to my knowledge.

Mr. MEEKS. Okay.

Mr. YAYLA. Not the Parliament members, but Baskan Saban Disli, deputy general director of AKP, was reported—Major General Mehmet Disli was reported to be among the coup makers. And, in fact, Akar testified that he put a gun on his head to sign off to a coup statement. However, strangely, when Akar was saved from Akinci Base, Mehmet Disli, Major General Mehmet Disli was with him arriving the Presidency, and on 16th morning, Mehmet Disli, Major General Mehmet Disli, brother of Saban Disli, the AKP deputy general director, arrived to the Prime Ministry with Akar, chief of staff.

Mr. MEEKS. Right. I am specifically focused on the Parliament right now.

Mr. YAYLA. That is the only connection I have.

Mr. MEEKS. Right. I want to know about that because, you know, that is part of democracy, because part of what I believe democracy also includes is elections, and there were parliamentarian elections in 2015, I believe. And I don't—you know, I think that we should change governments but via democratic elections, you know, like a President, like a Prime Minister, you know, member of Parliament, you remove them by elections, and so that becomes tremendously important to me.

Let me also ask, because I am trying to make sure that I understand what, if any, differences there are, particularly in dealing with journalists, A, are the journalists freely able to report on the failed coup and the aftermath and what took place in Turkey, and B, how would you describe how journalists—or the differences between how journalists are treated in Turkey as opposed to Russia?

Ms. OGNIANOVA. Well, the answer to the first question is a plain and simple no. They are not freely able to report on the coup or on any other sensitive issues. Turkey had been using overly broad antiterror laws for months before the coup, but now there is, plain and simple, no independent and opposition media to be voicing an alternative version of events to what the government is broadcasting happened during the July events.

As I said before, more than 100 media outlets were shut down directly after the coup. And these figures, the 100 detained, the 46 broadcasters shut down and accreditation taken, are merely a snapshot that were taken a couple of weeks after the coup. The events on the ground are evolving, and unfortunately to the worse for journalists. So chances are there are many, many more journalists detained.

But, as far as we know, there is no alternative voices that are available on the ground at the moment, minus the social media, Twitter, which has also been under attack——

Mr. MEEKS. Attack.

Ms. OGNIANOVA [continuing]. In Turkey.

And in regard to the comparison with Russia, well, in the months before the coup, I personally had made this comparison between the tactics that President Putin had been taking in regards to the Russian media for the past 10 years and what Mr. Erdogan had been able to achieve in a matter of a couple of years. In 3 or 4 years, Erdogan and his government were able to achieve the level of censorship in Turkey and Turkish media that the Russian Government had been able to achieve within 10 years.

Mr. MEEKS. Okay.

Let me ask Mr. Stein, how have coups in Turkey's past affected Turkey's relationship to the United States and within NATO? And how do you see this failed coup playing out in relation to others?

Mr. STEIN. I think this coup attempt differs because it wasn't successful, you know. And so what you had is a group of military officers who did not succeed in their mission, which was, I think, first and foremost, to decapitate the government.

And because of that, because of the purges, I think you will have an effect on the Turkish-NATO relationship, largely because general fear or sort of skepticism about Western institutions is very high in Turkey right now. A lot of the forces involved in the Istanbul component of the coup attempt were part of NATO's, you know, rapid deployable force. And so it breeds a conspiracy theory that NATO must have also known about the coup beforehand. And so, when you begin to lose officers who were exposed to NATO, you know, were operating within NATO, obviously, it creates friction between the two.

And I would say, just generally, when there are large-scale purges going on in any institution, people operating in those institutions are less free to speak their minds or to speak critically of, you know, their superiors. And so you will have a tendency within the armed forces basically to run everything up the chain of command so that you aren't, you know, sort of, accused of stepping out of line or stepping too far out of line. And so things will begin to slow down all throughout Turkey, at least in decisionmaking processes, and be made at the highest levels.

Mr. MEEKS. Thank you.

And my last question would be to Mr. Makovsky.

One of the things that I believe also sometimes threatens democracy is when countries get so nationalized, nationalism. So I would like to ask you, what are the consequences of the rise of Turkish nationalism?

And within that rise, are there any liberal voices calling for the protection of institutions regardless of the party in power? Let's remain that we need to talk to or get close to understand—get a better understanding of what is going on.

Mr. MAKOVSKY. Well, I think the primary consequence of the rise of nationalism is that it will make it extremely difficult, if not impossible, to repair relations between Turks and Kurds.

There had been a peace process. That peace process fell apart, actually, last year. And I think it is now clear, I think President Erdogan has made clear there will now be all-out war on the PKK.

And the, sort of, scorched-earth policies of attacks in the southeast will alienate the population, already has alienated the population.

But I think fighting the PKK has great support in Turkey. It always has. And, actually, I think—I know I refer to polls a lot, but there was one recently; which is the terrorist group that threatens us the most? And PKK was far and away number one; Fethullah Gulen, number two; ISIS, number three. I think that will be the primary result.

Are there liberal voices? Yes, there are still liberal voices. And I think particularly from the secular opposition party, center-left party, there has been a lot of criticism, particularly lately, about the purge. There was initially nationwide support for the purge, but lately the leader, Kemal Kilicdaroglu, of that party has been speaking out against its excesses and also, I think, speaking out against some of the excesses against the Kurds. So, there are liberal voices.

Also, I would just say, on the media, I don't think we ought to think it is North Korea. What it is is a very random process. There are still journalists you can read that criticize the government. I think if you look at the Hurriyet Daily News today, you will see a couple of op-eds that are critical of the government. The problem is the journalists never know when that pink slip is going to come. And so I—and, of course, they do a lot of self-censorship.

Thank you.

Mr. MEEKS. Thank you. Thank you very much.

Mr. ROHRABACHER. Colonel Cook?

Mr. COOK. Thank you, Mr. Chair.

Dr. Stein, going back to the military situation, the U.S. military is obviously caught between a rock and a hard place. And this anti-American—how about all the dependants? Is there a restriction now on American military personnel, their families being outside the wire, so to speak, where, before, you could visit the whole country and anywhere, right? Isn't that in effect right now?

Mr. STEIN. Yes, it is.

Mr. COOK. And the same thing with Incirlik? Even though we have a lot of military operations, everything is under the total control of the Turks in terms of airspace and everything that goes on there?

Mr. STEIN. That is also correct, yes.

Mr. COOK. Yeah.

And you kind of alluded to it. Yeah, I know it is a NATO ally, I know everything like that, but we have to face reality. If they want to shut down all U.S. American operations tomorrow, they could do it because they control everything.

The comment I made about the F-35s, do you have any reaction to that question that I refer to? Your feelings? Yes? No? Maybe?

Mr. STEIN. I think Turkey is—it is a Tier 3 partner in the program and has obviously invested money on it. And they will host both the maintenance facility, I believe, for the engines inside Turkey and are producing fuselages for the program. So, yes, I think it should be approved.

Mr. COOK. Even with the fact that getting that technology, their new friends are the Russians? Why not just give it to the Chinese or sell it to the Chinese, which is the rationale why we are developing that weapon, right?

Mr. STEIN. I think it is important to distinguish between, say, the Russians-Chinese potential adversaries and a NATO ally, so—but I do think that there are frictions over sort of the——

Mr. COOK. Okay. Sometimes we get it mixed up. Snowden stopped off in China; then he went to Moscow. So maybe I am old and I get them confused sometimes.

I am very, very, very worried about the Kurds. This is our ally. We had talked about them. We have deserted them in the past, with the history of Middle East. And it is like, here we go again.

And, yeah, they have been—and I see it is not going to be just the PKK, I think. Quite frankly, I think they are going to kill a number of them because of the population demographics and the fact that they can have a political influence, and this is obviously the opportunity to finally eliminate the Kurds as a political threat once and for all.

Do you agree with that premise?

Mr. STEIN. No, I don't. I think that they took a different tactic between 2013 and 2015 to try and reach political concessions. But one—the previous, Mr. Meeks' question about the rise of nationalism and perhaps poor decisionmaking by elected leaders is that you can lose touch with your population and then you can have a return to insurgency in the southeast, and I don't see a way out of that. But, no, I don't think that the plan is to eradicate the Kurds in Turkey.

Mr. COOK. Well, not completely, but to the point where they are not going to be a viable third party in Turkey. I believe it is 11 percent. Correct me if I'm wrong.

Mr. STEIN. I believe at the last election it was 10.7, about 11 percent, yes.

Mr. COOK. And the threshold is 11, right?

Mr. STEIN. Yeah.

Mr. COOK. And you don't think there is going to be any type of discrimination to push them over the border or eliminate them, almost similar to the Russians in Chechnya in terms of some of their policies?

Mr. STEIN. No, I don't think so. Although if their poll numbers do drop below 10 percent, you could have the AKP government contemplate early elections.

Mr. COOK. Okay.

Last question, I guess, going back to Russia. You know, a year ago, those of us in the NATO arena, we were worried about the snap exercises, flying in over Kaliningrad, everything like that. And the three countries that a lot of the NATO theorists thought would destroy the NATO alliance were Estonia, Latvia, and Lithuania; Latvia because they have such a high number of—Jerry is looking at me—Russian speakers.

And now I am saying here is a golden opportunity for Putin to grant his wish, and that is to destroy the NATO alliance. And you would not suggest that right now, instead of concentrating on those nations—this is a golden opportunity for Putin to finally separate, get Turkey out of the NATO alliance. For all intents and purposes, I think he would destroy it.

No comment? Anybody?

Mr. STEIN. I do think that there are parallels between Putin's current strategy versus how the Russians have historically approached, say, you know, East Germany during the cold war and exactly why it is important to lean in and continue to engage with Turkey and perhaps with——

Mr. COOK. No, no. I meant in relation to Estonia, Latvia, and Lithuania.

Mr. STEIN. I can't comment on that.

Mr. COOK. Okay.

Anyone? No one agrees?

Okay. I think I am used up. I yield back. Thank you.

Mr. ROHRABACHER. Thank you, Colonel.

I will just note, from everything that I have read about the F-35, well, maybe we should give it to the Turks at this point. We wouldn't necessarily be doing them a favor, from what I understand.

Mr. Weber?

Mr. WEBER. I think you have Mr. Connolly.

Mr. CONNOLLY. You are up because I am not on the subcommittee.

Mr. ROHRABACHER. You are on the committee.

Mr. WEBER. If I had known that, I would have written down some questions.

Mr. CONNOLLY. I can take the time and then come back.

Mr. WEBER. Go ahead. I am good with that.

Mr. ROHRABACHER. Mr. Weber yields to Mr. Connolly.

Mr. CONNOLLY. I thank my friend from Texas.

I am here both as a member of the House Foreign Affairs Committee and as the co-chairman of the Congressional Caucus on Turkey. I happen to believe that the U.S.-Turkey relationship is a very strategic and critical one. It is not one that can be dispensed with. I also happen to believe that it is in Europe's interest to see ultimate Turkey integration with the West and with Europe.

However, I share the concern of the chairman and my colleagues that President Erdogan, in his desire to consolidate power after a thwarted coup—and, by the way, the thwarting of the coup had universal sympathy. It had political sympathy in Turkey among the opposition parties. It had virtually complete sympathy here, in the West. It was condemned by all the right people. And in a very short period of time, politically, by overreaching, it would seem that President Erdogan has actually lost sympathy.

And I am very concerned about crackdown on the press, crackdown on political dissent, crackdown on political opposition, and, of course, using the coup, perhaps, as a pretext to get at any and all Gulenists, real or perceived.

And, Mr. Makovsky, I know that the chairman was going to give you an opportunity to talk a little bit more about Gulen, and I would welcome anybody else.

But I met with a Turkish delegation recently, and, from my point of view, look, the rule of law applies to you and to us. And you don't get to demand someone's extradition as some kind of symbol of our undying support. The burden is on the Government of Turkey to present evidence that would meet any reasonable legal threshold to justify the extradition of any individual, including Mr. Gulen, no matter how unpopular he may be in your ruling circle. And the fact that we don't do that in no way can be construed or should be construed as lack of support of this government for your government.

I wonder if you would comment on that. Because I was alarmed by the seeming lack of appreciation for what, to us, is a fairly simple legal precept. And you can expand on Gulen, with the consent of the chair.

Mr. MAKOVSKY. I completely agree with you, Congressman. I think it has been difficult for the Turks to understand—and those who do in the leadership understand have certainly not tried to educate their public—that this process is about hard evidence. And just as you said, if the hard evidence is there, then almost certainly Mr. Gulen will be extradited.

As I understand it, this process is primarily done in the Justice Department. They decide if it is worth sending to the courts. If the courts decide he is extraditable—I mean, there can be an appeal process, but assuming that he is deemed extraditable, the State Department has final sign-off. And the State Department has the right to make sure, before signing off, that he will receive a fair trial and humane treatment. But that is the basic process. If the hard evidence isn't there, he cannot be extradited.

Look, I just wanted to say something regarding the movement, the Gulen movement itself, because it is very hard to separate now discussion of post-coup Turkey from a discussion of the nature of the Gulen movement.

I think there are two very positive and significant hallmarks of the movement that distinguish it from a lot of Islamic movements, particularly radical movements that we have become very familiar with in this century and earlier, and that is they established a lot of schools that focused on subjects like math and science instead of religion, and they preached a message of peace and tolerance and interfaith comity.

That said, however, I think there is now a strong set of circumstantial—circumstantial—evidence that Gulenists have used the institutions of the Turkish state in order to pursue their enemies. This was particularly true with—or is widely believed to have been the case with the judicial actions against primarily military officers and other seculars in 2008 through 2010. And many innocent people, now free, now the conviction has been overturned, but many innocent people suffered and went to jail because of that.

I think there is some strong reason to believe that Gulenists were involved and were driving the process. That said, the fact that followers of Mr. Gulen may have been involved in such things or even in the coup doesn't make Mr. Gulen himself guilty. And I think that is what has to be decided through the evidence presented by the Turks in the extradition case.

Mr. CONNOLLY. I thank the chairman and my good friend Mr. Weber for their courtesy.

Mr. ROHRABACHER. Do you yield back to Mr. Weber?

Mr. CONNOLLY. I certainly do.

Mr. ROHRABACHER. Mr. Weber, you are recognized.

Mr. WEBER. Thank you.

Would you slide his questions over here to me?

Dr. Stein, you said in your comments, if I understood correctly, that it was hard to put your finger on why Turkey was so important abroad. Is that what you said?

Mr. STEIN. What I meant is it is hard to point to one single thing. You know, you can replace air bases, you know, but it is hard to replace the idea of a strong transatlantic relationship. And so it is that nebulous idea of strong transatlantic ties that makes Turkey most important.

Mr. WEBER. Okay. Well, let me do it this way then. How about if we just use one word, "geography"?

Mr. STEIN. That is a good word.

Mr. WEBER. Okay. So you would agree that, if for no other reason, their geographical location is fairly strategic?

Mr. STEIN. Absolutely.

Mr. WEBER. Okay. I rest my case, Your Honor. I thought so. I mean, it is extremely important, especially with Syria and all of the unrest. We need that ally. And, of course, I could go into energy pipelines and the finds in the Mediterranean Sea and the islands of Cyprus and just on and on and on. But Turkey is a very, very strategic, in my opinion, country that we need to be absolutely sure we take every necessary step—reasonable step to keep them as friendly to the United States as we can.

Having said that, I think it was—pronounce your last name for me, ma'am.

Ms. OGNIANOVA. "Ognianova."

Mr. WEBER. "Ognianova"? Okay. I think it was you who said that you began your daily chronicle of the problems with the media in March 2016.

Ms. OGNIANOVA. That is correct.

Mr. WEBER. Are you a Turkish citizen?

Ms. OGNIANOVA. No, I am not a Turkish citizen, nor am I an American citizen, but I have been covering Turkey since 2012. And what I said in relation to that daily documentation was that I wanted to stress when we were compelled to start a daily chronicle of coverage on Turkey. We have always covered Turkey, like any other country——

Mr. WEBER. From 2012?

Ms. OGNIANOVA. I have covered Turkey since 2012. CPJ has been covering it for years and years on end.

Mr. WEBER. Okay.

Ms. OGNIANOVA. It came on my personal purview in 2012, and since then, we have been covering Turkey very regularly. But this March, we were compelled to start a daily chronicle——

Mr. WEBER. Okay.

Ms. OGNIANOVA [continuing]. On press freedom in Turkey.

Mr. WEBER. But you would readily admit that those kinds of abuses of power had been going on for years.

Ms. OGNIANOVA. Oh, absolutely. They have been going on for years. But it was this year that they reached catastrophic proportions——

Mr. WEBER. Okay.

Ms. OGNIANOVA [continuing]. And we were compelled to start covering press freedom issues daily. We basically became a wire service for press freedom on Turkey on a daily basis in March.

Mr. WEBER. Were you doing it from inside the country or from afar?

Ms. OGNIANOVA. Well, we are headquartered in New York, but we have a correspondent——

Mr. WEBER. I am talking about you personally. And I don't mean to pry, if that is okay.

Ms. OGNIANOVA. I am the coordinator of the program, so in my program, apart from Turkey, I cover 30 other countries. But——

Mr. WEBER. But you aren't in Turkey itself.

Ms. OGNIANOVA. I go to Turkey every year. But our correspondent on the ground is the one who feeds us the daily chronicle of events.

Mr. WEBER. Okay. And——

Ms. OGNIANOVA. He is the reporter on the ground.

Mr. WEBER. Okay. And I think you mentioned later in the discussion that there are still some reporters or some media that still criticize the government, but they are kind of self-regulated?

Ms. OGNIANOVA. Well, there are individual journalists and some news outlets on the margins that do that, but they do that at an enormous personal risk. They could be prosecuted at the whim of the government at any time. And now that we have the state of emergency, the——

Mr. WEBER. The stakes are much higher.

Ms. OGNIANOVA. Absolutely. And all the Parliament or judicial scrutiny is gone for this——

Mr. WEBER. Forgive me, but let me break in. I don't want to run over too much time.

Ms. OGNIANOVA. Uh-huh.

Mr. WEBER. Not that some others haven't.

Would you say that the number of media organizations has gone from 300 in 2012, for example, to 50? Can you give me those numbers?

Ms. OGNIANOVA. I can tell you how many were purged. More than 100 in a matter of 2 weeks. Those are the hard numbers.

Mr. WEBER. Okay. When was that 2 weeks?

Ms. OGNIANOVA. Two weeks after the coup attempt.

Mr. WEBER. Oh, in that——

Ms. OGNIANOVA. We registered more than 100 being closed down. Since then, there were more that were closed down, but we captured that statistic 2 weeks after the coup.

Mr. WEBER. Okay.

Dr. Stein, I am going to come back to you. In your discussion with Colonel Cook, I think you mentioned that there is anti-U.S. sentiment. Would you say it was building before the coup attempt, or was that primarily since the coup attempt?

Mr. STEIN. The United States has never really been all that popular inside Turkey, so levels of anti-American sentiment has always been high. But, you know, it has reached new levels. It is levels I have never seen before. And, you know, things that escape detection, you know, prominent people on their sort of equivalent of cable talk shows going on television every single night and pointing to CIA involvement——

Mr. WEBER. Did that grow when Erdogan, in the last, say, 6 years, since he has begun to dismantle the constitution?

Mr. STEIN. I would say it has grown most heavily in the past year with the breakdown of the peace process and our actions in Syria.

Mr. WEBER. Okay.

I am concerned about the military base established in 1951, 3,300 acres in an area—Incirlik? Is that how you say that?

Mr. YAYLA. "Incirlik."

Mr. WEBER. "Incirlik"? In an urban area of 1.7 million people. The colonel alluded to that, them being inside, I guess, the compound proper, the base. Are they in danger?

Mr. YAYLA. Are they——

Mr. WEBER. Are the military personnel there on our base, are they in danger? Yes, sir. Go ahead, Dr. Yayla.

Mr. YAYLA. I believe they are in danger. And the reason for that is that after the coup, per Erdogan, media finger-pointed Americans so harshly that people on the street, because they cannot feed themselves with other free media, started to believe that the coup was really carried out by the American soldiers, with their support.

Mr. WEBER. Okay.

Now, somebody else said that—was it Twitter was under attack? How so?

Ms. OGNIANOVA. In the many cases of detentions of journalists, prosecutions of journalists, those detentions have happened in retaliation for tweets, not simply articles published or broadcast.

Mr. WEBER. It is not the Twitter company, per se, but whoever is doing the tweeting.

Ms. OGNIANOVA. Whoever is doing the tweeting is being prosecuted, detained, et cetera, but we have to say that Twitter, as a company, has censored a number of accounts——

Mr. WEBER. Okay.

Ms. OGNIANOVA [continuing]. On the questions and requests of the Turkish Government.

Mr. WEBER. Okay.

Ms. OGNIANOVA. And we are now trying to figure out why they have done that.

Mr. WEBER. So we are losing civil rights hand over fist.

Now, Fethullah Gulen, but all accounts—one of you said it—is teaching multiculturalism, diversity, and he is going some good work in terms of schools. Is that you all's general consensus, the panel here?

Dr. Stein?

Mr. STEIN. He is not new in Turkish society. And I think the allegations that he is an insidious character in Turkish society has been around since the 1970s, and that is why the purges have such wide-scale support.

Nobody really likes him because, while he does good work because he does set up charter schools, sometimes violating our own laws in terms of fair hiring practices, he is widely believed to be instructing his followers to infiltrate Turkish institutions to try and remake the Turkish state.

Mr. WEBER. Dr. Yayla, do you concur with that?

Mr. YAYLA. No, I don't, but it is very difficult to talk about it because, as soon as I speak, I am going to be labeled as Gulenist. But, however, I have to speak the truth.

I spent years on the ground to fight against terrorism, and I raided several thousand apartments for that because of the 9-1-1 calls saying that or tipping that there are terrorists in those flats, especially in Ankara. And this happened on several occasions. And with those raids, we raided several Gulen flats where students were staying, deemed from the outside as terrorists.

I have never, or my people, my officers, never found anything to incriminate in terms of violence. However, if it was a terrorist organization flat, there was always evidence.

Mr. WEBER. Oh, absolutely.

Mr. YAYLA. And then I think Gulenist people came out in regards to radical Islam and to jihadi terrorism, especially after 9/11 and with the ISIS, as the strongest voices against terrorism. Gulen himself was one of the few persons who came out and said——

Mr. WEBER. Right.

Mr. YAYLA [continuing]. That a terrorist cannot be a Muslim, a Muslim cannot be a terrorist.

Mr. WEBER. Let me move over here to Mr. Makovsky, but before I do, you had a son that was arrested?

Mr. YAYLA. Yes.

Mr. WEBER. And what is his status?

Mr. YAYLA. My son was arrested when he was leaving legally from the borders. Because my passport was canceled, I——

Mr. WEBER. He is still under arrest?

Mr. YAYLA. He is still under arrest. And he was released. As soon as he was released, he was rearrested in front of the prison again.

Mr. WEBER. Okay. And how long——

Mr. YAYLA. The only charge is being my passport is canceled.

Mr. WEBER. Has that been since July 15th?

Mr. YAYLA. Oh, yeah. After I wrote an article saying that I don't believe this was a real coup.

Mr. WEBER. Well, we wish him the best——

Mr. YAYLA. Thank you.

Mr. WEBER [continuing]. And hopefully he will be able to get out.

Mr. Makovsky, do you agree with the statement that, generally speaking, Gulen is viewed as doing some pretty good things?

Mr. MAKOVSKY. You are talking about within Turkey?

Mr. WEBER. Well, we would say—over here—well, let's just—you make an interesting point. Here and in Turkey.

Mr. MAKOVSKY. Look, as I said, he is, I think, viewed by many people—because of the nature of the schools and the teachings, he is viewed by many people here as something hopeful, a hopeful sign——

Mr. WEBER. Okay.

Mr. MAKOVSKY [continuing]. In the Islamic world. In Turkey, there has been, I think, widespread criticism of him. He was initially——

Mr. WEBER. More so since July 15th?

Mr. MAKOVSKY. Well, absolutely.

Mr. WEBER. Okay.

Mr. MAKOVSKY. He—if I could——

Mr. WEBER. So Erdogan has, you would argue, perhaps, has been successful in making him part of the scapegoat.

Mr. MAKOVSKY. Yeah, he has been demonizing him. And there is no doubt that there is a vendetta, particularly since December 2013——

Mr. WEBER. Okay.

Mr. MAKOVSKY [continuing]. As we discussed earlier.

Mr. WEBER. Let me move on, I am way over, if I may.

And can I just call you Nina?

Ms. OGNIANOVA. Yes.

Mr. WEBER. Do you agree with that assessment?

Ms. OGNIANOVA. Well, I haven't seen any evidence against——

Mr. WEBER. But you are reading all the tweets.

Ms. OGNIANOVA. And I think that we should come from the presumption of innocence and everyone should be innocent before proven guilty.

Mr. WEBER. Sure.

Ms. OGNIANOVA. And that has been the biggest issue with this crackdown, is that it is continuing without us having seen any evidence against these detainees.

Mr. WEBER. Well, with how many prearranged warrants did one of you say? There was how many people were arrested within a couple of days?

Mr. ROHRABACHER. Hours.

Mr. WEBER. Hours.

Ms. OGNIANOVA. I mean, hundreds of warrants, but——

Mr. WEBER. Right.

Ms. OGNIANOVA [continuing]. In terms of journalists——

Mr. MAKOVSKY. July 16th, the very next day, 2,745 judges were arrested.

Mr. WEBER. And, you know, if you do the math on that, if you signed a warrant a minute, that is 2,500 minutes, okay?

Ms. OGNIANOVA. I mean, no wonder that now the prisons are being cleaned of actual convicted criminals so that there could be enough space for the detainees after the coup plot.

Mr. WEBER. Yeah.

Ms. OGNIANOVA. I think what is really important is to note that the cancellation of passports is a critical issue at the moment. And many, many civilians have been canceled, their passports—journalists, civil activists, and their families, like we see in the case of Dr. Yayla. And we should be very vigilant about that. The U.S. leaders should not recognize these canceled passports.

Mr. WEBER. Well, thank you. I am way over time.

Thank you, Mr. Chairman.

Mr. ROHRABACHER. All right.

Now, to bring this hearing to a close, we are going to ask Mr. Meeks, any questions he has about the Gulenist movement, but anything else and to have a wrap-up statement.

Mr. MEEKS. Well, I don't have any specific question about the Gulenist movement. I think that it is a complicated scenario.

I think the entire relationship and where we are with Turkey is very, very complicated. When I look at the scenario and this nationalism, I know, the passion of nationalism generally also creates emotionalism, whether it is in Turkey or whether it is in the United States or wherever it may be.

I do know that we have a firm commitment to make sure that wherever, in Turkey, in Russia, in the United States, whether it is violation of human rights, where we don't have freedom of the press, where we don't have sound institutions, we have to speak out. We can't be silent about that. We can't just allow it to go.

That does not mean that we want to be enemies or anything of that nature. That means we want the same things for all people— human rights, freedom to determine your own self-determination. And when any of those things are not happening, I think we need voices to speak out loudly and clearly.

And if you don't feel—you know, for me, not equating the two, but what is great about the United States, in my estimation, is when I have a scenario like Colin Kaepernick, that he has the freedom to express——

Mr. ROHRABACHER. His ignorance.

Mr. MEEKS [continuing]. His—well, you say it is his ignorance. It is the freedom of this country. Because if you say Turkey, they will say it is ignorance also, with something that we disagree with, and that is why it is complicated. But you should have the freedom to express yourself, because people feel differently.

I mean, for example, for us, our number-one enemy is Daesh, or ISIL, because we feel threatened by them. To the Turks, it is the PKK, because they feel threatened by them. So we can't self-impose how they feel and say, well, you should feel exactly the way we feel, and if you don't feel the way we feel, you are wrong. Nor should they. And that is kind of where we are.

And I think Mr. Stein said, yes, geography does have a lot to do it. Yes, the fact that they are NATO allies has a lot to do with it. Yes, because we want to make sure that we are not condemning the entire Muslim population has something to do with it. If you have moderate Islamic countries, we want to make sure that we are engaging with them. We don't want to get rid of them. That is why it is important and why I think also, in the United States, we have Muslims, we have Christians, and they all should be welcome.

So my summary is, there is a lot of work and thought and negotiations that have to happen here. This is not a simple matter of you are right and you are wrong. It is a matter, though, that I think is unquestioned, that the number of individuals that have been arrested and detained and the journalists is a violation of human rights, that they are entitled to hearings and jurisprudence and should be returned, and it should not be something—that is something that is wrong. And we have to speak out about that loudly and clearly even if they are an ally, but also understand that we would be doing this because we want to work together, and our relationship is so important that we have to figure this thing out.

And I thank the witnesses for your testimony.

Mr. ROHRABACHER. Thank you, Mr. Meeks.

And I will just—a couple short questions, and then I will do a little wrap-up.

In terms of the Gulenists, let me ask—so far, it sounds like you are the only one who believes that the Gulenists, or at least some Gulenists, are involved with a nondemocratic approach to power, meaning being willing to be part of a coup and things such as that.

We will go with—first, let's ask Mr. Stein.

Mr. STEIN. I won't speak for the other panelists, although I presume that others probably think——

Mr. ROHRABACHER. Well, I am going to ask them too.

Mr. STEIN [continuing]. Like I do.

I think the Turkish people think that. And I think it is important, if we want to understand how they are——

Mr. ROHRABACHER. What are your—you are a specialist. Do you believe that the Gulenists were the organizing force behind this coup?

Mr. STEIN. I can't speak to that because I haven't seen any evidence to that.

Mr. ROHRABACHER. So you don't know——

Mr. STEIN. But were they infiltrating Turkish institutions? Absolutely.

Mr. ROHRABACHER. Okay. But you don't know, and that is your answer to that question.

Mr. STEIN. I don't know because the events of July 15th have not been told in full detail.

Mr. ROHRABACHER. Okay. Okay. Whatever the reason. I mean, you are an expert in a lot of these areas, including this, but there is not information enough for you to have made up your mind on that.

Mr. STEIN. No, I haven't seen anything.

Mr. ROHRABACHER. All right.

How about you, Mr. Yayla?

Mr. YAYLA. I don't believe that Gulenists were behind the coup because I have worked with several high-level generals in the military in the field, and most of the generals and high-level commanders in the military are known for their strong secularist approaches, and many of them do not like or hate Gulen. So I don't buy that.

Mr. ROHRABACHER. Okay. So it is no.

Mr. MAKOVSKY. As I tried to explain earlier to Mr. Connolly's question—perhaps I did so fairly inarticulately—I agree with Dr. Stein that there is strong circumstantial evidence that Gulenists have infiltrated, tried to infiltrate the——

Mr. ROHRABACHER. But that is not the question.

Mr. MAKOVSKY. The question is just about the coup?

Mr. ROHRABACHER. That is correct.

Mr. MAKOVSKY. I think we know nothing at this point about the coup. And I——

Mr. ROHRABACHER. Okay. So we don't know. So your answer is you don't know because we don't know enough about—and you don't know if the Gulenists were involved in the organizing the coup or not. Okay.

Ms. Ognianova?

Ms. OGNIANOVA. I absolutely concur with Mr. Makovsky.

And I also want to add that the persons who are qualified to make investigations and independent investigations in the media about the coup plot are now intimidated into silence. So, not only don't we know what happened, but those who are able to help us know more are either incarcerated or exiled.

Mr. ROHRABACHER. So I see we don't know, but one of the reasons we don't know is because the government is cutting off information sources to give us an accurate assessment, whether or not even the charge.

However, we do have one person, one witness today, Mr. Yayla, who served as a high-level intelligence officer in the police and in terms of confronting terrorism, and he has a long history involved and says that he does not believe the Gulenists were involved in organizing the coup. So, we have that as the answer for that question.

In general, do you see—look, obviously, the Gulenists are trying to be portrayed as a conspiratorial organization.

By the way, do Gulenists go to a particular church or mosque? Do they do things in public? They just have private meetings, that is it?

Mr. MAKOVSKY. That is my understanding. I have asked Gulenists this question, and they said they do not pray at their own mosques. So that adds to sort of the aura of mystery——

Mr. ROHRABACHER. Right.

Mr. MAKOVSKY [continuing]. For many churches. No one knows exactly——

Mr. ROHRABACHER. Well, I know that we had a problem in our country with a group of people who had an interesting philosophy; they were called Masons. And early in our country's history, there was this Masonic conspiracy that was supposedly around. But I looked at it, and I have read history—I am a history major, and I have done a lot of reading on it. George Washington was a Mason and all the rest of these people. And it seems to me what they had was a group of people who have shared values. And although they were private and did not make everything public, it was far from a conspiracy to try to take over governments, et cetera. Although, Masons had a lot of influence here—not enough influence to justify overthrowing George Washington and his government, because George Washington was a Mason.

We also today we have determined that before the coup attempt we already had signs of tyranny and repression and, even more important, corruption in Erdogan's government, perhaps leading all the way up to Erdogan himself. The fact is that, before there was reporting on that corruption, Erdogan himself did not seem to have any trouble with the Gulenists. But the Gulenists felt obligated to report it, knowing it would break their camaraderie, their tie to the man in power.

That indicates something good to me; that doesn't indicate something bad to me. That indicates that you have people who are courageous enough, knowing that their children could be arrested, even, by what appears to be someone who is becoming a megalomaniac. That sounds like a courageous group of people to me. Although they say there are people who are in parts of groups like this who are good people and bad people. Maybe there are some bad people too. We don't know.

But I think that the fact that Turkey and the Turkish Government was clearly involved with repressing opposition prior to the coup and, immediately after the coup, arrested thousands and thousands of people, many of whom could not have possibly had anything to do with the coup, suggests to us that today we have to be very concerned about the nature of Mr. Erdogan's government.

If he wants to use this as an excuse to eliminate real democratic rights of his people, if he wants to use this as an excuse to perhaps sever bonds with the West he is so upset with or whatever, if he uses this as an excuse to, for example, call off elections, to end the democratic things right—as if there is a state of emergency right now, that there is an army of Gulenists at the door ready to take over the country, so, thus, we have to arrest more people and shut up more newspapers. And this is—it is not only unacceptable, but it is also a historic disaster for the people of Turkey.

And, again, let's go back to the fundamental, and that is the people of Turkey have been good friends of the United States. We need to be concerned about them. And we need to basically not only pray for them, if we are religious, pray for them and that they come out of this, but also do what we can to at least ease this government over into the right direction.

And we can't do it by not admitting the challenge that we have, however, we can't do it by trying to cover up the fact that Erdogan—and, by the way, so when did Erdogan break with the Gulenists? When they started reporting on corruption that directly affected his entourage in government. So this is what everybody needs to know.

Now, with that said, thank you all for testifying today. You know, we are having a crazy political year here in the United States.

Mr. MEEKS. We are?

Mr. ROHRABACHER. It is about the craziest year I have ever seen. And what is going on in Turkey and this—which will change everything. I mean, the alliance and the stability that we have had, if Turkey goes with more radical, more anti-Western forces that are at play in Europe, the stability that we have had is going to go right out the window. It is going to change the history of the world.

So let's pray that people who do believe in a more free society and acceptance and open societies and believe in peace and harmony with their neighbors, let's hope that these are the people that come to power not only in Turkey but throughout the Mideast.

So, with that said, this hearing is adjourned.

[Whereupon, at 4:10 p.m., the subcommittee was adjourned.]

APPENDIX

MATERIAL SUBMITTED FOR THE RECORD

SUBCOMMITTEE HEARING NOTICE
COMMITTEE ON FOREIGN AFFAIRS
U.S. HOUSE OF REPRESENTATIVES
WASHINGTON, DC 20515-6128

Subcommittee on Europe, Eurasia, and Emerging Threats, Dana Rohrabacher (R-CA), Chairman

September 13, 2016

TO: MEMBERS OF THE COMMITTEE ON FOREIGN AFFAIRS

You are respectfully requested to attend an OPEN hearing of the Committee on Foreign Affairs, to be held by the Subcommittee on Europe, Eurasia, and Emerging Threats in Room 2200 of the Rayburn House Office Building (and available live on the Committee website at http://www.ForeignAffairs.house.gov):

DATE: Wednesday, September 14, 2016

TIME: 2:00 p.m.

SUBJECT: Turkey After the July Coup Attempt

WITNESSES: Ms. Nina Ognianova
Coordinator
Europe and Central Asia Program
Committee to Protect Journalists

Mr. Alan Makovsky
Senior Fellow
Center for American Progress

Ahmet S. Yayla, Ph.D.
Deputy Director
International Center for the Study of Violent Extremism

Aaron Stein, Ph.D.
Resident Senior Fellow
Rafik Hariri Center for the Middle East
Atlantic Council

By Direction of the Chairman

The Committee on Foreign Affairs seeks to make its facilities accessible to persons with disabilities. If you are in need of special accommodations, please call 202/225-5021 at least four business days in advance of the event, whenever practicable. Questions with regard to special accommodations in general (including availability of Committee materials in alternative formats and assistive listening devices) may be directed to the Committee.

COMMITTEE ON FOREIGN AFFAIRS

MINUTES OF SUBCOMMITTEE ON _____*Europe, Eurasia, and Emerging Threats*_____ HEARING

Day___*Wednesday*___ Date___*September 14, 2016*___ Room___*2200 Rayburn*___

Starting Time ____*2:25 pm*____ Ending Time ____*4:10 pm*____

Recesses |__*0*__| (____to____) (____to____) (____to____) (____to____) (____to____) (____to____)

Presiding Member(s)

Rep. Rohrabacher

Check all of the following that apply:

Open Session ☑ Electronically Recorded (taped) ☑
Executive (closed) Session ☐ Stenographic Record ☑
Televised ☐

TITLE OF HEARING:

Turkey After the July Coup Attempt

SUBCOMMITTEE MEMBERS PRESENT:

Rep. Meeks, Rep. Brooks, Rep. Cook, Rep. Weber

NON-SUBCOMMITTEE MEMBERS PRESENT: *(Mark with an * if they are not members of full committee.)*

Rep. Connolly

HEARING WITNESSES: Same as meeting notice attached? Yes ☑ No ☐
(If "no", please list below and include title, agency, department, or organization.)

STATEMENTS FOR THE RECORD: *(List any statements submitted for the record.)*

N/A

TIME SCHEDULED TO RECONVENE _____
or
TIME ADJOURNED ____*4:10 pm*____

_____
Subcommittee Staff Associate